HOLLYWOOD

INVENTION WORKS:

Develop, Protect and Make Money With Your Invention

Richard Crangle
Crantec Research

All rights reserved. This book is protected by copyright. No part of this book may be reproduced, stored in a retrieval system, or transmitted in any form or by any means, electronic, mechanical, photocopied, microfilmed, recorded, or otherwise, without written permission from the publisher or author.

Copyright © 1999
Richard Crangle
Salt Lake City, Utah

Library of Congress Number: 98-94804
CIP

ISBN 0-9664835-1-0

Printed in the United States of America

Richard Crangle
President and Founder

CRANTEC RESEARCH

Adjunct Professor

UNIVERSITY OF UTAH
SALT LAKE COMMUNITY COLLEGE

Dedicated to those who have had continued confidence in my quest to develop innovative technologies over many years.

Table of Contents

Preface..ix

I. Introduction To Technology Research and Development: Historical Uses, Common Needs And Future Demands of Innovations   1

    A.   Historical Use and Misuse................1
    B.   Common Needs & Future Demands...14

II. Patents: An Overview   25

    A.   Legal Basis…..........................…..25
    B.   Definition and Subject of a Utility Patent: Summary..........................27
    C.   Patent Application Structural Requirements.............................…...27

III. Legal Requirements For Obtaining A Patent   31

    A.   Patent Applicants........................…....31
    B.   Tests for Patentability 31
    C.   Timely Filing of Patent..................36

IV. Patent Process and The PTO   37

    A. Formal Procedures..........................37
    B. Structure of PTO...........................37
    C. PTO Responses and Actions.............38
    D. Fees: Filing, Issuance and Maintenance................................40
    E. Conception, Reduction To Practice, and Interference............................42
    F. Design and Plant Patents................44

V. Patent Infringement   49

    A. Damages......................................49
    B. Elements and Consequences of Infringement................................51
    C. Grounds and Remedies for Patent Infringement................................57

VI. Technology Innovation Act   61

    A. Purposes......................................61
    B. Past Innovation Funding..................65
    C. Remedies to Improve Technology Innovation..................................68
    D. Shared Research, Development, Financing and Royalties.................72

VII. Prepatent Considerations for Research and Development — 77

    A. Documentation of Invention..............77
    B. Constructive Reduction to Practice....78
    C. Interference Practice........................78
    D. Meeting with a Patent Attorney.........79
    E. Disclosing Information to an Attorney...79
    F. Avoiding a Conflict of Interest...........80
    G. Preparation for Meeting with a Patent Attorney................................81
    H. Prepatent Options Available..............83
    I. Confidential/Nonconfidential Disclosures......................................89
    J. Initial Marketing..............................92
    K. Maintaining Invention as a Trade Secret......................................93

VIII. Licensing or Sale of the Invention — 99

    A. Types of Licenses............................99
    B. Royalty Payments and License Fee Basis............................101
    C. Sale of a Patent.............................103

IX.	**Filing for Foreign Patents**	**105**
	A. Time Restrictions..........................105	
	B. Foreign Patent Applications............105	
	C. Absolute Novelty Requirements........108	

X.	**Conclusion: A Response to Change**	**111**

Appendix   **117**

- Endnotes......................................A-1

- Bibliography and Table of Cases and Authorities...............................B-1

- U. S. Patent & Trademark Office Fee Schedule..................................C-1

- Process and Methods Patent.............D-1

- Mechanical and Material Patent..........E-1

- Biotechnology and Methods Patent......F-1

- Design Patent................................G-1

- License or Sale Checklist..................H-1

Preface

Invention Works is directed toward providing information needed by those involved in new technological development, including scientists, managers of technology-based businesses, CEOs, educators, board of directors, financial officers, research and development companies and inventors. Because of the complexity in the development of innovative technologies, specialized knowledge is needed across a broad range of issues relevant to successful technology outcomes. The costs are great and the penalty for failure is often harsh. As J. B. Quinn, a professor at Dartmouth, stated in his article *Technological Innovation, Entrepreneurship and Strategy*

> . . . for success, the individual must be fanatically committed in order to endure the pain, frustrations and effort of overcoming the technical and market obstacles that always confront a new idea.

One can quickly add "financial challenges" which must be overcome throughout the research and development process.

Even market research itself discourages innovation as in the case of the copy machine, whose inventor, Chester Carlson, was told for 17 years that there was simply no market for his invention.

Despite these perils the demands for new technologies to sustain and improve life across the spectrum, and the rewards of even small successes, create an urgency to continue the quest. Thomas Edison toiled for 10 years and experimented with over 4,000 filament materials to achieve success with the incandescent light bulb. That he continued undaunted in the face of numerous disappointments was, in part, a function of his drive and conviction that one could learn from each of those failures, even though each one seemed to be a "granite wall 100 feet high and 10 feet thick." The result was no less monumental than discovering fire for the second time which transformed the entire world from one heated and illuminated only by fire. With the multiplying imperatives of the present age pressing upon us from all sides, it is a necessity to succeed in our individual and collective endeavors to provide the essentials of existence for an enormously increasing population with its attendant impact on the natural resources, the environment, health care and a multiplicity of other social concerns. This book was written with the goal of making technology innovation more efficient, more prolific and more successful for more people.

While the Intellectual Property/Patent sections are specific, *Invention Works* is not intended as a patent-it-yourself book but rather to serve as an informational context which interfaces with the invention development process. Not all patented technologies are commercially or socially successful and many successful products are not patented or are not even patentable.

Broad issues relevant to technological innovations are addressed in related areas of business, economics, law, science and politics. Patents are not spontaneously generated without the diligent application of science and/or technology; similarly, replicated scientific data or technologies when reduced to practice do not happen without the mobilization of intellectual, political and economic capital. All of these interconnected disciplines have a history and have been shaped by various historical events and forces, many of which are covered in the first chapter and noted throughout the text. The form and function of innovative technology and the work of protecting it operates in a historical milieu of which those involved in the research and development business need to be aware. It is hoped that a focus on these critical matters will provide significant help for those wanting to produce good and useful innovations to improve the world and to achieve a successful outcome for their noble quests.

"We live forward; we understand backward."

– William James

I. Introduction To Technology Research And Development: Historical Uses, Common Needs and Future Demands Of Innovations

A. Historical Use and Misuse

Technology is an essential part of human life, even a fundamental characteristic of human nature which provides power to potentially move people forward. Because of its complexity and long-term impact, it can be better understood by assessing the results after the fact. As a term of art coined in the late eighteenth century, *techne* combined with *logos* became a formal discipline after millennia of being an inchoate and often chaotic process of misguided trials, catastrophic errors, and episodic successes. Engines of war ranging from the catapult through Greek fire and nuclear weapons have killed users and targets alike. Some devices to supply energy, such as the windmill, were mere toys for a thousand years and have become major power machines with little danger to people, places or things.

Other energy technologies such as the steam engine, whether used for its original purpose as by its inventor, James Watt, to drain mines in England, or for production or hauling products with steam locomotives, exploded and became a major cause of conflagrations and pollution of the environment. Electrical energy, gasoline engines and nuclear plants did the same. Solar energy has not yet had a real chance. Whatever the source of power, the machines powered were viewed both as a menace to and a liberator of humanity. The automobile, which transformed transportation in the twentieth century and redefined personal mobility, was declared "inherently dangerous" by the court in *MacPherson v. Buick* as early as 1916, yet was eagerly endorsed by the consumer. Airplanes have regularly fallen from the sky since Kitty Hawk but have also transported billions of people over trillions of miles. While the hue and cry over the downside of technology were heard long before the Luddites attacked the steam-powered cloth looms in 1811, the collective concern for the negative impact of technology on the citizen, and society in general, has continued.

While science and technology continued to develop along separate routes and according to different methodologies, both began an expansion in scope to encompass some of the common concerns of the human condition, *viz.*, food, clothing, shelter and health care. From a historical perspective, two of the Horsemen of the Apocalypse, pestilence and famine, became moving targets of technological application although war continued to preempt most technological innovation and application. Two seemingly mundane innovations of the early medieval world, the horse collar and the stirrup provided improvement to both food production and militarism. The horse collar which distributed the weight of the load over the chest and shoulders of the draft horse allowed for the cultivation of the more heavy soils and bottom land of northern Europe and enabled the draft animal to haul much heavier armaments and munitions. The stirrup provided a superior platform for the military knight engaged in battle mounted on his horse. As a tangential result, riding horses became easier with stirrups and encouraged the use of horses for transportation. Generally, a dynamic social system in any era needs to meet urgent demands, which require focused and decisive actions directed toward specific outcomes. To do nothing or to engage in dysfunctional tasks causes the system to malfunction or to stop. Technologies, and the research and development needed to generate them, are at the center of the most dynamic societies. These societies are directed toward sustaining and improving many forms of life and the environment, expanding the global economy, and augmenting political power.

The quest to set these essential technologically-based systems in place has taken many forms and has undergone a variety of permutations over centuries. During the hunter-gatherer stage of human evolution, technology was oriented largely toward devices and tools to achieve those ends. Political power issues were narrowly directed toward securing and defending food sources. With the advent of an agrarian way of life, supplanting hunting-gathering as a predominant way of life, technology shifted to develop more efficient methods of slashing and burning to improve the fertility of the soil and to develop implements to plant, cultivate and harvest. Several thousand years after the emergence of slashing and burning, the first patent issued by the newly established U. S. Patent Office in 1790 was for a process to make potash from burned foliage for soil enrichment. Organized militarism was established for conquest of new lands and defense of those already claimed; technology was enlisted to produce a wide range of military munitions.

As fiefdoms were built on conquered lands, the ensuing suppression of the masses of people saw the equivalent suppression of technological development for food, clothing, shelter and "common works" to enrich the quality of life. Instead, physical, mental and financial resources were primarily used for the construction of colossal edifices for kings, clergy and grandiose campaigns of conquest. In Western Europe, between c.1066 - 1300 C.E., more stone was quarried and used for cathedrals and castles than in all the prior Western European eras combined.

In this milieu, paradigms were carved in stone and rarely shifted; the concept of the global village was nearly an oxymoron. Technology was clearly the slave of those in power, a power which approached the absolute in many cases and gave rise to nearly absolute corruption in many sectors of society. This condition provided additional evidence for the summary statement of Lord Acton in the nineteenth century that ". . . power tends to corrupt and absolute power tends to corrupt absolutely." Under this kind of political and economic control, the arts and sciences were dependent upon the *noblesse oblige* of wealthy patrons and technology, too, subsisted at the sufferance of capricious patronage.

An emerging view, that certain individual values and rights were irreducible and inalienable, was given impetus by the Enlightenment movement during the eighteenth century. In terms of the impact of science and technology, priorities began to shift toward utilizing these disciplines for purposes other than the aggrandizement of the elite and powerful. The proposition that every person has inherent value and self-worth helped direct the scientific and technological focus more broadly. In combination with a more egalitarian view of society gaining more credence at the end of the eighteenth century and pressures created by a growing population, innovations useful to a larger portion of the population began to appear. The technological equivalent of the scientific Copernican Revolution was aided by the development of more sophisticated machines in various areas of human enterprises, including communication with Guttenberg's printing press in 1449 C.E. Built on a used wine press, printing immediately began to preempt the laborious work of monastic scribes in the production of books and other documents. This caused the proliferation of the written word, thereby ushering in the era of publication and the incipient information age. This has continued unabated and, along with the development of electronic information platforms, contemporary society continues to be transformed.

Rather than serving or even pandering to an elite of power and wealth, both science and technology shifted to become beneficial to a wider variety of classes. In place of technology directed primarily toward military ends and colossal buildings, technology took on new roles. Those roles included making innovative devices and processes to confirm new scientific theories such as Kepler's powerful telescope to aid in the confirmation of the heliocentric hypothesis advanced by Copernicus and Galileo in the mid-seventeenth century. This transition was neither easy nor pleasant. Despite the bold and elegant discoveries of Galileo and Copernicus, the pathway through ignorance, arrogance and dogmatism was perilous, even brutal. This is evidenced by the execution of Giordono Bruno in 1600 C.E. under the authority of the Inquisition. He was burned, while tied to a post, wearing an iron mask tightened over his face to prevent him from speaking to the crowds about the reasons for his execution: the heliocentric theory and pantheism. In addition to confirming theories and hypotheses, innovations such as the microscope in the hands of Robert Hooke allowed visualization of living cells for the first time, thereby providing a new model to understand the composition of living things.

Progress was slow and, in many ways, a first century Roman lived better and healthier than a resident of London, England, in the middle of the nineteenth century. Neither knew the cause of diseases; neither knew how to prevent them. In 1850, surgeries were done without anesthesia; infant mortality was nearly 15% during the first year of life;

and longevity was still approximately forty years. As one of the earliest pioneers of systematic epidemiology, Dr. John Staunt compiled longitudinal studies in the mid-seventeenth century showing the average mortality rates of London residents wherein 25% were dead by age 6; 40% by age 20; 65% by age 36; and 90% by age 42. Even creative and dispositive research showing that scurvy at sea could be prevented by the consumption of citrus fruit by sailors was suppressed by the British navy for nearly fifty years. Imbalanced humours of the body were still purged by various purgatives, including bloodletting, and infections were without remedy. Technology, after the invention of the printing press, still neglected health care and favored the advance of machines of industry and war until the middle of the nineteenth century. While the science and art of medicine were developing in most European universities, technological developments languished during and long after the inception of systematic medical research. The retardation of medical health care technologies over 400 years, c.1450-1850 C.E. helped contribute to a general living condition in Northern Europe and its colonies reminiscent of Thomas Hobbes' *Leviathan*, which described the lives of humans in the "state of nature" as ". . . solitary, mean, nasty, brutish and short."

Significant reasons for the stunted status of medical art and science can be traced to a thousand years before the printing press. Beginning with the collapse of the Roman Empire in 476 C.E., medical research and learning took two distinct paths, one east, the other west. The eastern schools of medicine were established by the Arabs; the western pathway led into Western Europe. The two met five hundred years later at the medical school at Salerno, Italy. Astonishingly, both eastern and western medical learning relied heavily, and in the west slavishly, on the tradition of Hippocrates c.550 B.C.E. and Galen of the second century C.E. While the Arabic medical schools made some small innovations in medical practice, medical theory was largely in the form of compilations of traditional texts which in the case of Rhazes' tome weighed in at 22 pounds, and was a compendium of antidotes, nostrums, potions and practice described by the ancients.

Little was done to improve either the practice or theory regarding surgery and clinical care in both schools of medicine. Part of the reason lay in the view that surgery, surgeons and the practice of surgery were considered inferior to other medical procedures and protocols. This is the consensus found in the leading compilations of those centuries. Rhazes' *Canon*, Avicenna's *Canon of Medicine* and Albucaris' *Collections* all consider surgery to be a "vulgar" pursuit, the "least desirable alternative," and suitable mostly for tradesmen, such as barbers, who essentially used the same tools to shave a beard as to cut for bladder stones, peel cataracts, lance tumescent tissue, cauterize a wound or amputate a limb. Ubiquitous infection was the almost inevitable concomitant to surgery such that pus itself was thought to be essential to healing any wound. In a summary fashion, the *Collections* simply described surgeries as only two kinds, ". . . those which benefit the patient and those which usually kill him."[1]

A similar form of resignation is pervasive even more systematically throughout western medical literature between c.476–1100 C.E. The fate of medicine in Western Europe was primarily in the hands of monastic scribes who succeeded in preserving the works of Hippocrates and Galen. Without the aid of experimentation which was inhibited by ecclesiastical authorities and without outside resources, medical innovations were virtually nonexistent; medical practice, theory and healthcare fell into desuetude. The dominant view characterized as "Asklepian," substituted ritual, ceremony and resignation to cosmic forces instead of experimentation, scientific and technical research, development, inductive and deductive reasoning and the use of empirical data. This orientation, combined with reluctance to perform medical experiments and the chilling effect of tradition, resulted in suspended animation for medical art and science until the Renaissance. While the paradigm shift was noticeable in various technological sectors and during various time periods, the momentum increased dramatically beginning in the seventeenth century. Some of the early seeds of experimentation sown by avant-guard medievalists, such as Roger Bacon in the thirteenth century C.E. were cultivated by seventeenth and eighteenth century experimenters and innovators in a broad range of endeavors in the natural and medical sciences. It is remarkable that the eyeglasses produced, based on Bacon's optical experiments, were disseminated throughout Europe and Asia within thirty years.

The technology of the natural sciences grew more quickly and more dramatically than the technology of medicine, food production, shelter or transportation. It was not until the pioneer work of Lister and Pasteur that a new paradigm based on germ theory was understood and acted upon in the second half of the nineteenth century. It took nearly another century before penicillin, accidentally discovered in molds, was used to treat bacterial infections, one form of germ which was visualized under a sixteenth century microscope now greatly amplified by electricity. Despite primitive use of vaccinations for viral infections such as smallpox in China c.300 B.C.E., and some sporadic efforts to inoculate during the late seventeenth century, such as the inoculation of Benjamin Franklin's children by Dr. Benjamin Rush, virtually nothing was done in this area until the twentieth century.

In order to significantly shift either the scientific or technological paradigm, there are various factors needed to allow innovation to emerge in place of what Thomas Kuhn calls the "normal science" in *The Structure of Scientific Revolutions*. Typically, Kuhn observes, entrenched, self-serving, financially invested and institutionalized entities resist paradigm shifts and favor even dysfunctional "normal science" over functional innovation. It has been unusual for institutional entities to willingly set aside "normal science" and incur the risks associated with innovations, despite the presence of urgent need, anticipated demand, profit potential and social benefit.

B. Common Needs and Future Demands

Because the overwhelming megatrends over the centuries have shown established institutions to be resistant to paradigm shifts, thereby inhibiting innovations, societies have had to look to the individual innovations in science and technology for new paradigms, hence, new discoveries. However, the present and future challenges are unprecedented in their complexity and costs. This makes innovation and implementation of new products to meet urgent needs even more daunting.

As a perennial need, food production requirements are sharply rising just to maintain the current inequitable world allocations which leave over 65% of the world population undernourished and 15% in a starvation status. Without predicting the Malthusian inevitability of mass starvation, but to avoid global starvation, food production needs to also nourish the projected increase in population in the next decade, which increase will be larger than the entire world population existing in 1955. In addition, this needs to be accomplished without poisoning the environment with pesticides, herbicides or fertilizers; and it needs to be done without sacrificing animal populations, either by destroying their habitats or by killing them outright. In terms of abating our massive population from outstripping food resources, innovative birth control methods, high-yield grain production and other means need to be developed and utilized to provide a countervailing force to world-wide overpopulation and poverty. It remains to be seen if scientific and technological innovation by individuals is possible on this massive scale or if the individual innovator must rely more on entrenched and resistant institutions. If so, one of the threshold challenges will be effecting rapid and fundamental paradigm shifts in an atmosphere of "normal science."

The need for energy sources brings this issue into sharp focus. Assuming a conservative 7% annual increase in energy requirements to power more and larger engines of all kinds, energy needs over the next decade and a half will exceed the total energy produced in all of human history. However, fossil fuel sources are becoming increasingly scarce, more difficult to locate and much more expensive to produce. In 1950, the average oil well could be drilled for $50,000; in 1995, the average exceeded $4,000,000 or a 6000% increase. Because of these escalating costs, the energy fields have largely been monopolized by giant multinational corporations, rather than entrepreneurs. Despite the costs, the major energy producing corporations have produced huge profits but have produced almost nothing in the form of viable alternative energy sources. Likewise, with a multitude of consolidations in the U. S. automobile industry, only two major corporations remain from over 3,000 small manufacturers during the past century. However, the auto industry has done little to reduce fossil fuel consumption to power vehicles, produce alternative energy-powered vehicles or reduce toxic emissions.

It is an open question whether or not an individual innovator can bring about significant paradigm shifts in an arena dominated by megacorporations which may have an interest in resisting change and maintaining the economic status quo. On the consumer side, it remains an unanswered question whether users of dominant transportation technology are responsible enough to curtail the dangers inherent in high velocity fossil-fueled vehicles and to distinguish between real needs and endless wants. The Federalists' suspicions of the masses if translated into a question of technology would ask: Do the masses have the capacity to manage the technology already at their disposal? The masses would ask: Do rulers or *cognoscenti* have the capacity to regulate technology?

Significant innovations are urgently needed in the areas of waste disposal in an era where environmentally compatible landfills and incinerators are nonexistent or inadequate and pose real dangers, including hazardous waste disposal, which has increased arithmetically over the past 50 years and is predicted to increase geometrically in the next 25 years.

Economically, technological innovations are needed to generate a substantial portion of the increase in real capital available world-wide to support a growing global population. To simply sustain the economies of the world at their present inadequate levels in both the rich and poor nations, requires more than doubling the present amounts of capital over the next ten years. This has to be accomplished in spite of world-wide chronic scarcity with relentless escalation in tax burdens imposed by governmental entities which distribute the wealth according to governmental agendas which often bear little resemblance to the needs or will of the people. Parenthetically, the issue of governmental regulation of industries is still unsettled in that a growing body of research suggests that the very governmental agencies established to regulate these industries have been "captured" by the industries themselves. This "capture theory" is especially plausible when applied to the very large and very wealthy corporations which dominate certain industries and which use economic machinations to influence, even control, governmental agencies.

Increasing significant tax assessments imposed by most European countries and other industrialized nations to fund a broad range of programs are being imposed at similar levels in the United States. During the next two decades, there will be an urgent need to create at least 50% more jobs. Jobs created in the past decade, as well as the present, are mostly service related, typically paying minimum wage or slightly higher. Technology-based jobs have generated less than 20% of the new jobs in the industrialized nations over the past decade. Most projections are flat over the next decade without the emergence of significant technological innovations to alter these stagnant trends, and without creating large scale displacement or gross exploitations which lead to violence and war.

Within this context, even maelstrom, of real human needs, protection of intellectual property (hereinafter IP) in technological innovations developed to meet these needs is one which has played an increasingly important role, especially within the past two centuries. While there had been IP protection granted under sovereign enactments and at common law in the United States prior to establishing the U. S. Patent Office in 1790, this protection was sporadic at best and was often based on arbitrary and capricious decisions, usually to enrich royal favorites. IP protection emerged to include a variety of patents, trademarks, service marks, copyrights, and trade secrets. Prior to codification under the U. S. Patent and Trademark Office (hereinafter PTO) enactments and regulations, IP protection was based on a longstanding body of property law.

Essentially, one "owned" a right in IP on the model of one owning real estate or chattel. One who "infringed" on such an owner's right was viewed as a "trespasser on the case" or a thief and was subject to fines and/or imprisonment, pursuant to common law penalties for these violations. While the penalties were commensurate to the harshness of the legal system in many areas of the law, an aggrieved party still needed to enter the labyrinthian common law system with all of its risks, costs and surprises. Jarndice v. Jarndice, recounted by Charles Dickens in the nineteenth century, serves as an illustration of the quagmire of the common law system in practice wherein the parties were totally exhausted by the protracted litigation. These countless perils encountered in the common law system gave rise to the warning that "at common law, one had a wolf by the ears." It was the legislative intent of the Colonial Continental Congress to establish a patent department to provide protection to inventors and authors in an orderly, timely and systematic manner and to reduce the need to engage the common law system. The first United States Patent Statute of 1790 established the U. S. Patent Office to provide a protection to the inventor, and also to give a measure of security to inventors in the research and development of patentable inventions. As a property right, IP gives a patentee a claim against the "whole world." The patentee also entered into a contract with the United States Government for an exclusive-monopoly of a specific invention under specific terms and conditions which included the obligation of the patentee to disclose the invention to the "whole world."

The secrecy of a technology-based guild system was relinquished for a patent system; however, the legal, economic and political basis of the PTO was not without its detractors. A vigorous dissent was lodged by the well-known Benjamin Franklin, a politician, businessman, researcher of many technologies, and the inventor of the Franklin stove, the rocking chair and bifocal spectacles, among others. Speaking for himself and other like-minded persons, Franklin argued that all inventions should be donated to the public at large and should pass into the public domain, rather than establishing a federal agency to protect individual interests. It was recognized that Franklin's contingent may have had the luxury of affluence on its side and could afford to donate inventions to the public. On the other hand, this position gave an advantage to the large manufacturing and distribution corporations which could preempt and dominate a technology field by mobilizing large amounts of capital, thereby creating its own "monopoly," based on the "iron law of economics" or the workings of the "invisible hand," rather than on the limited monopoly granted to a patentee. As a concession to Franklin's opposition to the PTO, the federal government has never subsidized the PTO with any tax funds and it is the only federal agency which has been and is self-supporting from fees paid by the inventors or their assignees.

Issues originally raised during the debates concerning the establishment of the PTO are still alive and are the source of tension two hundred years later. Some assignee companies, in a deliberate strategy to prevent others from obtaining a patent, will publish research studies and development reports on technologies in journals. Rather than carrying out the apparent altruistic objective of Franklin's position, these companies preclude competition in a technology area by making it impossible for the competition to gain property or contractual rights through the patent process.

Another alternate strategy which limits access to patent protection and its commercial advantages is to delay publication of research in scholarly journals or to avoid dissemination of reports of technology development. This trend has been noticed especially within the past four to five years, whereby publication of research and development pertaining to a wide range of technologies is being delayed more than 6 months after discovery, in order to gain a commercial advantage. This is particularly problematic in the interface among academic institutions, private sector businesses and governmental entities. It remains to be seen if the challenges of the present age to maximize the benefits of technological innovation to meet human needs can be addressed through the patent process with the contrived chilling effects caused by these trends and others yet to come. In order to better evaluate and assess these issues with particularity, the structure and function of the patent process itself needs to be addressed.

II. Patents: An Overview

A. Legal Basis

The patent laws and procedures for obtaining patents have developed through both legislation and litigation. During litigation, existing laws are applied and further defined, and set precedents for handling future cases. Each source has been influenced or controlled in various ways by the other. While court cases are ongoing, there have been major pieces of legislation from which the patent process has evolved. Starting with the U. S. Constitution, the patent owner (patentee) is granted a monopoly pursuant to Article 1, Sec. 8:

> Congress shall have power . . . to promote the progress of science and useful arts, by securing for limited times to authors and inventors, the exclusive rights to their respective writings and discoveries . . .

In order to carry out this constitutional mandate, Congress, through the PTO, grants limited monopolies to inventors in the form of patents in exchange for full disclosures of their inventions. These limited monopolies are potentially in conflict with anti-trust laws; therefore, the activities of patent owners are scrutinized to be sure that they stay within the legal confines of patent rights when they make, use or sell their inventions.

A United States patent is a negative legal right in the sense that an owner of a patent may prevent others from making, using and selling the patented invention within the United States and its territories. There are certain unusual cases where the patent owner is not allowed to make, use or sell the patented invention, such as when a patent is dependent upon or embodies a second patent which is held by someone else who refuses to grant a license or will not allow use of the second patent. If an invention is deemed to be a threat to national security or is immoral, the government may prevent a patent from being issued. Contrary to popular belief, ideas, facts, natural laws and mathematical equations cannot be "inventions" and are deemed nonpatentable by the PTO.

Since a U. S. patent is limited to the United States and its territories, an owner of a patent cannot use that patent to prevent others from making, using or selling the invention in a foreign country. However, if the invention was manufactured in a foreign country and imported to the United States for use or sale, it would be an infringement of the U. S. patent and could be prevented, even though the invention was made outside the United States.

A patentee generally has the right to make, use and sell the patented invention, as well as the right to license one or more entities to do the same. These rights continue for twenty years from the date the patent application is filed if a utility patent is issued, or for fourteen years for a design or plant patent.

B. Definition and Subject Of A Utility Patent: Summary

The invention of a utility patent can be a product, process or apparatus for making a product. Since 1981, the PTO has allowed patentability for "living things." In 1988, a patent was allowed for a transgenic mouse which contained a variety of genetic material found in other animals.

C. Patent Application Structural Requirements

By carefully following application procedures and requirements, potential problems will be minimized or avoided, and will eliminate unnecessary delays. A utility patent application is comprised of three parts.

1. <u>Drawings</u>.

Drawings are placed at the front of the application.

2. <u>Claims</u>.

Claims define the metes and bounds of the invention embodied in the product, process apparatus. The claims should be listed in progressively more narrow manner from the preamble as it transitions to the body of the claim. Claims fall into two general categories independent and dependent.

    a. An independent claim is one which does not refer back to a preceding claim. An example of an independent claim is as follows: Claim 1 - An electromagnetic transmission device wherein audible radio waves are transmitted to a remote receiving component without wires.

b. A dependent claim refers back to another independent claim. An example of a dependent claim is as follows: Claim 2 – The device of Claim 1 wherein the audible volume can be regulated by means of a dial.

3. <u>Specifications and Disclosures</u>.

Applicants must disclose inventions in clear, concise and exact terms. To be patentable, an invention must be fully disclosed to the extent that the claims and specifications would enable one with ordinary skills in the trade or industry to actually make the invention so that it works. Moreover, the best mode needs to be set forth in the patent application in order to satisfy the statutory requirement of Sec. 112, which insists on specific descriptions that are "clear, concise and exact."

While the best mode is to be described in the patent application, this requirement obliges the inventor to give only the best mode which is known at the time to the inventor. Even the most complex invention involving chemical discoveries, processes, or an article of manufacture requires enabling specifications and explanations to allow those of ordinary skill in that industry to actually make the invention.

III. Legal Requirements To Obtain A Patent

A. Patent Applicants

The applicant(s) for a patent must be the person(s) who actually invented the subject of the patent application, not a business entity.

B. Tests for Patentability

The tripartite test applied by the PTO and the courts to any subject of a patent application is as follows:

1. <u>New/Novel</u>

    The subject of a patent application must be found to be clearly novel or original in order to meet the test of Sec. 102 of the Patent Act. If prior art discloses enough to be able to anticipate[2] or actually make the invention, the application will fail the novelty test. Generally, after the public has gained knowledge of an invention, the invention is declared not patentable because it is not new or novel.

Sec. 102 of the Patent Act requires that a prior disclosure must actually describe the subject of the patent application in order to preclude patentability of the invention. If this description is sufficiently complete to enable one skilled in the trade or industry to make the invention, the subject of the patent application is deemed not to be new or novel, hence, it is not patentable. In a word, novelty benefits the first person to invent.

2. Useful/Utility

The legal basis for utility, as a test for patentability, is derived from the useful arts statement in the U. S. Constitution, which was incorporated into Sec. 101 of the Patent Act. In particular, the test of utility goes to the issue of specific usefulness rather than general or speculative utility.

The so-called patent medicines of the nineteenth century would be an example of claiming nonspecific benefits and features for potions which purported to be panaceas for ailments ranging from arthritis to zygapophaseal pain and did fail the test of specific utility. More recently in *Brenner v. Manson,* 86 S. Ct. 1033 (1966), the courts denied a chemical compound patent application using the test of utility because there was no showing that the chemical composition actually worked.

3. Nonobviousness

The legal basis for the third test of patentability is found in the Patent Act, Sec. 103. This test was devised to help distinguish a true inventor from a skillful mechanic who might be expected to make ordinary advances in a trade or industry.

In a search for an objective test using general standards rather than *ad hoc* subjective tests, the courts used such legal constructs as "a flash of creative genius," as in the case of *Cuno Corp. v. Automatic Devices Corp.,* 315 U.S. 84 (1941). This language has since been rejected by the final paragraph of the Patent Act, Sec. 103 but still retains the demand that the invention, not the inventor, must be ingenious or creative.

In combination patent applications, the PTO and the courts have used the concept of synergism, wherein new results arise from a combination of old, i.e., known elements. For example, the court in *Sarkisian v. Winn-Proof Corp.*, 606 F 2d, 671 (1982), insisted with respect to combination patents that "there be an unusual or surprising result." A new combination of old or formerly nonpatentable components or processes may be patentable.

A recent biotechnology patent case illustrates how the PTO applies this test. Glenner was determined to be the true inventor, not Goldgaber, because Glenner had disclosed the amino acid sequence of AAP and its application to diagnostic assays. Glenner "supplies the key and the lock . . . Goldgaber only turns the key," which is obvious to one having ordinary skill in the area of molecular biology and the use of recombinant DNA techniques. This case is articulated in the Board of Patent Appeals & Interferences, *Golgaber ex parte* 11/8/96.

Nonobviousness is determined in a primary test measured by a hypothetical person who is thought to have ordinary skill in the particular discipline to which the invention pertains. There is a 3-step statutory procedure to determine the nonobviousness of a patent:

a. a patent search and survey of prior art and other relevant information available

b. an examination of the similarities and differences of subject patents *vis-a-vis* prior art, and

c. an evaluation of the level of ordinary skill in the trade or industry. The examination of the subject patent is neither strictly structural nor mechanical but functional as applied to the entire invention.[3]

The secondary tests applied to a subject patent application with respect to nonobviousness include commercial success, long-felt but unmet need in trade or industry, the failure of others over several years to solve a problem, the very existence of prior information, expression of disbelief by experts, and later improvements on the discovery. An articulation of these secondary tests can be found in *Graham v. John Deere Co.,* 383 U.S.1 (1966). An interesting historical example can be found in the actual process of "inventing" the self-scouring plow by John Deere in the 1840s.

It is important to note, however, that any one or two of these considerations alone would be insufficient to make a determination of patentability. An idea may be the basis of a successful commercial venture and/or may solve a long-standing problem but, by itself, it is not patentable. In this regard, patentability is not based on these considerations individually or even in the aggregate, but on the overall technological application of an invention which must pass all the primary and secondary tests relevant to the attributes of novelty, usefulness and nonobviousness.

C. Timely Filing of Patent

A patent application needs to be filed within one year from the occurrence of any one of the following events:

1. sale or license of the invention
2. offer to sell the invention
3. use of invention for commercial purposes
4. publication of your invention anywhere in the world.

If an application is not filed timely, the invention is never patentable.

IV. Patent Process And The PTO

A. Formal Procedures

Since the PTO functions as the U. S. Government's only agency to protect the patentee's rights, formal procedures are emphasized and required in the patent process. On an adversarial model, the patentee has the burden of proof to show the PTO that the subject of the patent application is patentable. Under 35 U.S.C.A., Sec. 115, there is a duty imposed on the patentee to show diligence and candor during the patent process. To do otherwise potentially precludes patentability.

B. Structure Of PTO

The PTO is divided into groups and subgroups based on the type of subject matter contained in the patent application. For example, one group may examine only chemical patents while a subgroup may examine biochemistry patent applications. In a subgroup or art unit, examiners may specialize in specific types of biochemistry applications.

Similarly, all issued patents are divided into classes and subclasses which can be utilized in a patent search. Once a patent application is received by the PTO, it is given a filing date, serial number and assigned to a class and subclass section. All information received by the PTO relevant to a patent application is treated as strictly confidential and cannot be accessed even through the Freedom of Information Act.

A patent application is processed in sequence according to filing dates unless designated as "special" because of its urgency for national security, energy-related reasons or because of special circumstances of the patentee who files a petition. Within 6-18 months after receipt of a patent application, the patent examiner will determine if the application is accurate and complete, and will examine the claims made and compare them to prior art or prior patents. On the basis of this examination, the PTO will respond to the patentee with a "first office action."

C. PTO Responses And Actions

The first office action response from the PTO gives the applicant information regarding the patent search and examination, reasons for acceptance or rejection of some claims, and requests for clarification or statements regarding any other deficiencies of the application. There are time-certain periods in which the applicant needs to respond to the PTO, which also includes an opportunity to petition for an appeal of PTO decisions.

While these communications may continue over an indefinite length of time, the PTO may exercise its prerogative after the second examination of the application and declare its determination to be final. This final determination of the PTO can only be overturned by successful litigation in a federal court. The legal presumption is that the PTO's decision is correct. This presumption can favor the applicant on an acceptance of claims or the issuance of a patent but it can also work against the applicant on final rejections. Under 35 U.S.C.A., Sec. 282, an issued patent is presumed to be valid and confers legal rights to the patentee. However, these presumptions impose a duty of candor upon the applicant; a breach of candor can invalidate an issued patent. Such a breach may be less than deliberate fraud or more than inadvertent negligence. Under the language of the Patent Act, the duty of candor is breached by "bad faith or gross negligence." 37 CFR, Sec. 1.56. In a leading chemical patent case, the court defined an invalidating breach of candor to be "calculated recklessness," as articulated in *W. R. Grace & Co. v. Western U.S. Industries, Inc.*, 608 F2d 9th Cir. (1979). In this case, the chemical compound essential to the invention did not work as described, and the applicant knew that material fact when filing the patent application and suppressed this information.

D. Fees: Filing, Issuance, and Maintenance

As of October 1998, the fee for filing a patent application is $770, unless the applicant qualifies as a small entity (100 employees or less), files a small entity affidavit and pays a reduced fee of $385. There is no other fee to be paid to the PTO during the patent pending period until a notice of allowance is sent to the applicant indicating that the patent is allowed and will be issued upon receipt of a patent issuance fee of $575. After issuance of a patent, maintenance fees are to be paid on or before 3.5 years, 7.5 years, 11.5 years, and 17 years after patent issuance, according to a changing fee schedule published by the U. S.

Patent Office, Washington, D.C. 20231 and found in the Appendix.

Several important changes in international patent law occurred with Public Legislation 103-465 which was enacted by the PTO on June 8, 1995, and implemented on January 1, 1996. These provisions included changing the long-standing 17-year term for a utility patent from date of issue to a 20-year term from the date of filing. A new provision allows for the filing of a provisional patent application for a filing fee of $150 or $75 for a small entity. There is no other fee associated with the new provisional patent application since it is abandoned by the PTO at the end of one year from the filing date. While a provisional patent application will not be examined, it does give the applicant a date-certain for domestic priority. This means that, in the event that more than one patent application is filed on the same invention, the first applicant to file would be considered the first inventor. It also allows the applicant one additional year if a patent is to be issued. This additional year can provide time in which additional research, development and financing can be accomplished. Unlike a utility patent application, a provisional application needs only a specification and a drawing but must meet the enablement and best mode requirements of Sec. 112. However, this type of application filed without claims will be scheduled for examination only after a regular and separate patent application is filed.

E. Conception, Reduction To Practice And Interference

When more than one inventor files a patent application on the same invention which is deemed patentable, the PTO can declare an interference. Rather than issuing two patents on the same invention, it is necessary to determine the first inventor who is to be issued the patent. Generally, the "first to invent" rule is applied, unless the application has been abandoned, suppressed, or concealed. See 35 U.S.C.A., Sec.102(g).

In practice, the application of this general rule is problematic since it involves a determination of which applicant first conceived the invention and which applicant reduced it to practice. The former refers to an event essential to the invention process which is established by laboratory notebook records, specific drawings, engineering plans or prototypes. Because of these necessary evidentiary elements needed in a PTO decision, it is critical that all material information be documented and preserved by the inventor. The strength of this accumulated evidence to establish conception of an invention replaces the "flash of genius" test which the PTO and courts used prior to 1952. From the conception of an invention through reduction to practice, due diligence is required of the senior or first inventor in order to prevail against a junior or subsequent inventor. The due diligence so required is measured and compared to the time of conception by the junior inventor.

Sr. Inventor → *Conception* → *Due Diligence* → *RT Practice*
Jr. Inventor → *Conception* → *RT Practice*

Conception of Invention by Senior Inventor

This schematic illustrates the relationship between the due diligence shown from the time of a junior inventor's conception of the invention. It also displays a significant rule that a junior inventor can only challenge a senior inventor if the junior inventor reduces the invention to practice first.

Reduction to practice is essential to the invention process and occurs either when a working prototype is built, or established with the filing date of the patent application. The former is actual reduction to practice and the latter is a constructive reduction to practice. Except for an application pertaining to a perpetual motion machine, the PTO does not require a working model of the invention to be sent with the patent application. However, the PTO can exercise its prerogative to demand a working model anytime after the patent application is filed.

F. Design and Plant Patents

Although design patents may have utility, their functions are separate from their design. Any claim in a design patent application for utility or functionality will preclude acceptance of a design patent application. Rather than drawings, specifications and multiple claims, the design specifications are presented as a single drawing or a set of drawings which disclose the invention. There is only one claim in a design patent application which is illustrated by the drawings. The tripartite test for a design patent is the following:

1. novelty,
2. ornamentation, and
3. nonobviousness.

It is instructive that criterion 3 uses the standard of "the ordinary intelligent man" *(sic)*. See *Schwinn Bicycle Co. v. Goodyear Tire & Rubber Co.,* 444 F2d 295 (1970).

35 U.S.C.A. Sec. 161 also allows patents for plants to be issued to one who

> ... invents or discovers and asexually reproduces any distinct and new variety of plant, including cultivated sports, mutants, hybrids, and newly found seedlings, other than a tuber propagated plant or a plant found in a cultivated state ...

Similar to the design patent, the claim in the specification of a plant application describes the plant shown by an illustration, drawing or photograph. The test employed includes novelty, distinctness and nonobviousness and is applied only to asexually reproduced plants, *e.g.,* using grafting, budding, cutting, layering or dividing, instead of using seeds. It does not need to be useful but it does need to be distinct. An issued plant patent grants the patentee an exclusive right to exclude others from " . . asexually reproducing the plant or selling or using the plant so reproduced." See Sec. 163.

While the plant patent is not new and was amended under the 1954 Patent Act, it has spawned a variety of derivative issues, some of which are not entirely settled. These include the extent of patent protection given to a wider spectrum of life forms such as bacteria, viruses, fungi, yeast and DNA-based genetic material. As mentioned earlier, a leading court challenge initiated in 1970 and finally decided in 1980, affirmed patent protection granted for an invention of an oil-eating bacterial microorganism. In this precedent-setting case, *Diamond v. Chakrabarty*, 447 U.S. 303 (1980), the court held that the plant patent system did not preclude patent protection for other forms of life. Since that decision, a wide range of life forms have been patented, including a transgenic mouse in 1988 which contained a variety of genetic material from other species such as chickens and humans. From this line of patentable inventions for life forms has emerged the rapidly growing areas of biotechnology and genetic engineering, resulting in the production of new life forms as well as the cloning of existing life forms.

V. Patent Infringement

Sec. 271 of the Patent Act clearly states the actions which constitute patent infringement:

> . . . whoever without authority makes, uses or sells any patented invention within the United States during the term of the patent, therefore, infringes the patent.

The remedies available to a patentee are also set forth in Secs. 283-295 of the Patent Act and include injunctive relief, damages and attorney fees. An injunction is ordered by a court of proper jurisdiction to prevent the violation of any patent rights of the patentee on terms deemed reasonable by the court. A directive to cease and desist making, using or selling a protected invention is essential to the injunction.

A. Damages

Damages for infringement are intended to compensate the patentee and usually stipulate a reasonable royalty from the date of first infringement. The court may impose treble damages as equitable compensation. Some damage awards have been very substantial in the area of infringement litigation, e.g., $55.8 million dollars awarded to Pfizer Medical Inc. in *Pfizer Inc. v. Int'l Rectifier Corp.*, 586 C.D. Cal. (1985); Hughes Tool Co. was awarded $134 million and $70 million dollars in interest in *Smith Int'l, Inc. v. Hughes Tool Co.*, 81 C.D.Cal. (1986). These awards have increased over the years and are sturdy warnings to those in research and development and technology businesses that efforts need to be made early on to determine the risk of pursuing a technology area which may result in patent infringement litigation. Moreover, patents need to be carefully drafted and precautions taken when disclosing technology and conducting business. Attorney fees may be awarded to the prevailing party only if the court deems it to be reasonable and equitable under certain circumstances. The award of attorney fees to the prevailing party is not automatic.

Most patent infringement cases in federal court result in civil penalties, such as monetary compensation for an infringement. However, the courts may exercise criminal sanctions involving the incarceration of the agents and officers of the infringing company. A recent case in the U. S. Court of Appeals, *Cochran Consulting, Inc. v. Uwatec USA, Inc.*, 96-1145 (1996) overturned a prior court's criminal contempt sanction of the defendant company for its refusal to produce a printed copy of the ROM Code used by the accused device. The criminal contempt sanction in this patent infringement case was pursuant to an injunction which prohibited the defendant company from the manufacturing, marketing, importing, distributing, servicing and selling of any product utilizing reading code memory. However, the appellate court found that the ROM Code in question was not actually patented by the plaintiff; hence, there was no infringement and the criminal sanction was lifted.

B. Elements And Consequences of Infringement

A test central to any infringement determination is based on the doctrine of equivalents which has meant that if the means and function of an alleged infringing invention are the same or equivalent to the elements of an issued patent, there was a presumption that infringement had occurred. In order to implement the test, the claims of both inventions are examined to determine if the claims of one invention substantially describe the claims of the other invention. Rather than simply concluding that if the claims are equivalent there is infringement, another doctrine is invoked to further corroborate the examination of claims. This doctrine is called a "file wrapper estoppel" which states that the claims of one invention were narrowed during the prosecution of the patent so that the allowed claims did not infringe on the other patent. The file wrapper refers to the entire file of the patent application, including the office actions taken, the inventor's responses, and the resulting parameters of the claims. Therefore, a claimant to the infringement litigation is "estopped" from arguing that the claims of its patent are actually broader than those allowed in the issued patent. In a word, a patentee is limited to the scope of the claims agreed upon.

This doctrine is of serious consequence in the research and development process, since the resulting technology may be limited in terms of patent protection if the patent application is filed too early or if more narrow claims are accepted before a technology is fully developed. Similarly, a patent may be vulnerable by being invalidated during an infringement proceeding, if the claims are overly broad and were not sufficiently narrow to prevent infringement by prior art.

A monumental historical example of this problem can be found in the Selden patent, a "pioneer" patent, which was issued in 1896 to protect the entire automobile technology. Selden filed infringement suits against any producer of automobiles and exacted sizeable royalty payments, until Henry Ford successfully overturned the Selden patent largely on the basis that the file wrapper disclosed that the claims were too broad and actually infringed on prior patents.

Combination patents present a problematic type of adjudication in an infringement litigation and have given rise to a multitude of difficulties owing to the complexity that can result from various combinations, especially chemical, pharmaceutical and genetically-engineered materials. In a combination patent, it is literally only the combination of elements which makes the invention patentable. If each and every element in one combination is substantially equivalent to each element in the accused patent, infringement can be sustained. For example, a combination patent may include elements A, B, C, D and E, and produce results Y. Another combination patent may include elements A, B, C and E and produce the same result Y, yet not infringe on the former patent. In a pharmaceutical application, the removal of the element D, which may cause a stomach upset, but decrease pain, is a clear advantage. In a leading case relevant to infringement of a combination patent issue, the court enunciated that if any element or its substantial equivalent is missing from the accused product or process, there is no infringement. See *Pennwalt Corp. v. Durand-Wayland, Inc.*, 833 F2d 931 (1987). This holding has come to be known as the "all elements rule" and has been used and enlarged upon by subsequent courts in addressing combination patent infringement. The court in another major litigation of a combination patent followed the "all elements rule" and articulated that where an element of a claim is entirely missing, there is no infringement. The statement made by the court in *Corning Glass Works v. Sumitomo Elec.*, 868 F2d 1257 (1989), in affirming the *Pennwalt* rule says:

> The "all elements rule" correctly states the law of this circuit adopted in *en banc* in Pennwalt . . . 'element' be used in the sense of a limitation . . .. An equivalent must be found for every limitation of the claim somewhere in an accused device . . .

These recent combination patent cases focus more sharply on the fundamental issues framed in *Graver Tank Mfg. Co., Inc. v. Linde Air Products Co.,* 339 U.S. 605 (1950), a precedent setting case decided almost fifty years ago. This case articulated the basic rationale of the doctrine of equivalents, as to its application to infringement litigation, and has been used as an authoritative reference for a half century. It cited a judicial and public policy need to protect an inventor from technology piracy, the need for specifically drafted claims, and the right of the public to legitimately design around patents. The last statement helps prevent an overly broad monopoly of a technology by one inventor and allows for incremental improvement patents which keep open all technology areas for innovation.

In supporting this long-standing rationale of the doctrine of equivalents, a later holding in *London v. Carson Ririe Scott & Co.,* 946 F2d (1991) helps clarify these issues:

> . . . designing or inventing around patents to make new inventions is encouraged, piracy is not . . . where one infringes, instead of inventing around a patent by making a substantial change, merely makes an insubstantial change, essentially misappropriating or 'stealing' the patented

invention, infringement may lie under the doctrine of equivalents.

To complete this analysis of the important issues surrounding the doctrine of equivalents, the court concludes by emphasizing the balance which needs to be struck when weighing inventors' rights with public policy.

> Intentional "designing around" the claims of a patent does not by itself constitute a wrong according to the doctrine of equivalents. Designing around patents is, in fact, one of the ways in which the patent system works to the advantage of the public in promoting progress in the useful arts, its constitutional purpose. Inherent in our claim-based patent system is also the principle that the protected invention is what the claims say it is, and thus that infringement can be avoided by avoiding the language of claims. It is only when the changes are so *insubstantial* as to result in "a fraud on the patent" that application of the equitable doctrine of equivalents becomes desirable.

These fundamental issues are still under scrutiny and apply to a wide range of recent cases, including combination patent litigation for chemical, computer, medical, and biotechnology patents.

C. Grounds And Remedies For Patent Infringement

1. <u>Statute of Limitations</u>.

Under 35 U.S.C. Sec. 186 (1982), the statute of limitations for filing an infringement action is 6 years, starting from the time when the patentee actually or constructively has knowledge of the infringement. The infringer must then be notified of its infringement.

2. <u>Importation of Patented Invention</u>.

Since 1989, the Patent Act, 35 U.S.C. Sec. 154 (1988) makes it a direct act of infringement to import inventions covered by a U. S. patent into the United States without authorization by the patentee or assigns.

3. <u>False Marking</u>.

Under 29 U.S.C. Sec. 292, false marking of an imitation product owned by a patentee without consent or license is deemed to be infringement. This section prohibits any false marking indicating "patent pending," "patentee" or any such false advertising and is subject to a fine of "not more than $500 for every such offense"; the patentee may sue for an additional penalty and damages. A patentee is also subject to penalty for continuing to falsely mark the invention with a patent marking when the patent rights have expired. In some cases, a product may be prematurely marked "patent pending" in the manufacturing process before patentability has been determined and continues to be so marked even after a product may be deemed unpatentable or the patent process abandoned.

4. <u>Arbitration</u>.

The Patent Act allows for arbitration of an infringement or dispute arising from a contract between parties pertaining to the patent rights. See Sec. 244. Specific procedures, awards and payments for arbitration are governed by Title 9, U.S.C. and are considered final and binding on all parties to the arbitration proceedings. Notice of the arbitration and its results are filed with the Commissioner of the PTO and are entered into the file wrapper as part of the prosecution record.

Notice must be filed in order for an arbitration award to be enforceable.

VI. Technology Innovation Act

A. Purposes

Pursuant to 15 U.S.C. Chapter 63, Congress enacted legislation in 1986 to promote and implement technological innovation and commerce because of the benefits to be derived by our nation and its citizens. The purpose of this Act is stated in Sec. 3702:

It is the purpose of this Act to improve the economic, environmental and social well-being of the United States and its citizens by

1. establishing organizations in the executive branch to study and stimulate technology;
2. promoting technology development through the establishment of cooperative research centers;
3. assimilating improved utilization of federally funded technology developments, including inventions, software and training

technologies by state and local governments and the private sector;

4. providing encouragement for the development of technology through the recognition of individuals and companies which have made outstanding contributions in technology; and

5. encouraging the exchange of scientific and technical personnel among academia, industry and federal laboratories.

To give a basis for this "purposes" section, the findings in Sec. 3701 include the following observations generated from the congressional task force on Technology Innovations:

(1) Government antitrust, economic, trade, patent, procurement, regulatory, research and development, and tax policies have significant impact upon industrial innovation and development of technology but there is insufficient

knowledge of their effects in particular sectors of the economy.

(2) No comprehensive national policy exists to enhance technological innovation for commercial and public purposes. There is a need for such a policy, including a strong national policy supporting domestic technology transfer and utilization of the science and technology resources of the federal government.

There is a multitude of examples from the annals of both science and technology history showing the economic benefit to a nation which researches, develops and commercializes significant innovations. In the modern world which disseminates technology more quickly than in past centuries, the economic advantages go to the nations which commercialize them for profit. As a technology matures through its initial "fluid phase" and "transitional phase" to its "specific phase," the nation which researches and develops a technology innovation may not always be the one which benefits most economically from its commercialization. To illustrate this, consider the proliferation of small electronic appliances such as radios, stereos, toasters, and television sets after their invention and production in the first two phases in the United States. These have benefited other countries, notably the Oriental countries, in the third phase of mass global commercialization. In order to meet the economic purpose of Sec. 3702 to benefit the United States, efforts need to be made to commercialize technology innovations in ways that result in ongoing monetary benefit for the U.S. In addition, social well-being and environmental impact need to be evaluated in the research, development and commercialization stages of new technologies. While the petroleum powered automobile may be one of the most innovative and widely embraced technologies of the twentieth century, its effect on the environment and the long term well-being of citizens is still an open question. Because of the enormous costs and other necessary resources associated with many innovative technologies, only a few citizens stand to realize the purposes stated in Sec. 3702 (1)-(5). Assistance is needed especially for smaller sized companies with limited resources. In order for small companies to enter certain areas of research and development, financial, scientific and technical personnel and laboratory support are needed throughout the innovation process.

B. Past Innovation Funding

This orientation is in sharp contrast to the research and development of expensive innovations of only a century ago wherein government entities were virtually absent from technology alliances and the funding process. A monumental pioneer innovation such as the incandescent electric light was very expensive over its nearly ten years of research and development and was financed by a private group led by J. P. Morgan, one of the wealthiest individuals of the nineteenth century. This occurred in an era in the United States prior to the Sherman or Clayton Antitrust legislation and prior to federal income taxation (1913). It was through private sector funding that this seminal innovation, the entire system of applied electricity, and the foundation of Edison General Electric Corporation were established.

In addition to substantial funding needed for the nascent incandescent light industry and its ancillary businesses during the research and development phases, continuing financial support was needed to combat strong resistance by the entrenched gas industry. Among other political machinations, the gas industry attempted to levy an additional charge of $1,000 per mile of electrical conduit and to launch a propaganda campaign broadly alleging that everyone in proximity to an electrical cable would be in immediate danger of electrocution. Because of these daunting challenges, and ongoing capital demands estimated to be the equivalent of several billions of dollars in contemporary buying power, it took twelve years after beginning production in 1881 to finally make a profit in 1893. This was the case despite ownership of a broad utility patent by Thomas Edison and his partners which granted them a legal monopoly for the incandescent lamp. This patent was issued just 3 months after the patent application was filed.

Innovations spawned by relentless creative inventors usually working alone or in small groups became the driving force for an unprecedented increase in technological productivity beginning in the United States after the Civil War. This model became the dominant pattern until the beginning of World War II, during which time military technology was developed under the auspices of the government and its agencies, and was often transferred into the growing laboratories of large corporations. Despite this taxpayer-funded technology windfall for the large corporations after World War II, many technologies languished and were even stultified within the confines of the corporations. For example, nuclear energy technology was given impetus because of its military applications. The Manhattan Project alone cost over two billion dollars to produce two nuclear bombs. However, it took over forty years for nuclear energy to supply more than 2% of the power needs in the United States. Even with such a mature technology and energy needs worldwide, the deficiency of adequate safeguards for nuclear plants led to Chernobyl, which is now a virtual metaphor standing for a technology disaster of colossal proportions.

There are two salient forces which militate against innovations within large corporations and retard technology. One is risk aversion; the other is bondage to institutionalized paradigms. These, combined with other factors, have resulted in a lag of technological innovation which is noted in Sec. 3701(5).

C. Remedies To Improve Technology Innovations

To remedy this serious deficiency and to " . . reduce trade deficits, stabilize the dollar, increase productivity gains, increase employment, and stabilize prices," See Sec. 3701 (6), federally funded research and collateral laboratory and scientific and technological support are recommended. These objectives are to be met specifically under the direction of a Technology Administration Office within the jurisdiction of the Department of Commerce which was established under the authority of the Technology Innovation Act. In addition to mandated collaboration with private entities in the United States, this Innovation Act of 1986 established a separate program and office in Japan to monitor technology innovations in that country and to translate and publish reports regarding Japanese scientific discoveries and technological innovations. This provision regarding Japan was included because of the prolific output of technology, the large number of U. S. patents being issued to Japanese-based firms, and as an effort to reverse the disproportionate one-way flow of technology from the United States to Japan. As a politically-based policy, it was in part a trade-off for trade policies favorable to Japan.

As a further effort to alleviate the deficiencies in U. S. technological innovation, Cooperative U. S. Research Centers are to be established under Sec. 3705 of the Act. Such centers are to enter into cooperative agreements with educational institutions or other nonprofit organizations to develop a "generic research base" which can benefit industry. These cooperative alliances are also to include provisions for the allocation of patent rights to those participating in the centers and for *pro rata* shares of license fees and royalties which may result from technology transferred to licensee companies. Within this framework, the centers would be partially self-sustaining and could parlay some of the license proceeds into future technology development and for scientific research. Grants are to be limited to 75% of the total cost of the project and "any person or institution may apply to the Secretary of Commerce for a grant or a cooperative agreement available under this section." See Sec. 3706. The National Science Foundation is authorized to provide financial assistance in the form of nonrenewable planning grants to universities or nonprofit institutions for Cooperative Research Centers and to assist in the administration and management of the projects selected.

When useful technology is researched and developed through these agencies with the allocated resources, Sec. 3710 addresses the ways and means of transferring the innovations to state and local governmental entities and into the private sector for federally-funded research and development. Pursuant to this directive, adequate staff is to be funded under this section and not less than 5% of the total budget specified is to be used to implement the technology transfer function through the Offices of Research and Technology Application. In addition, ways and means are to be set in place to disseminate the appropriate information to the private sector, including collaboration with other federal agencies, *i.e.*, the National Science Foundation and the Federal Laboratory Consortium, and to utilize databases or create a mechanism to inform interested persons in the private sector. However, it is not clear what person, group or entity in the private sector will receive the first opportunity to access this technology, share the personnel, or what terms and conditions will cause these transfers to take place. It is within these areas of ambiguity that allegations of political influence, cronyism, and self-serving technology transfers have been made. To provide further communication between federal laboratories and the private sector, in part, to reduce the aforesaid kinds of problems, Sec. 3710 (e) (1), *et seq.*, states that actual training courses, relevant information, materials, and seminars for small businesses and industry will be provided to heighten awareness concerning these federally-funded programs and, at least, to make these opportunities known to a broad range of citizens. Included in this section are specific guidelines and directives for proper cooperation among the various agencies, personnel and laboratories with respect to allocation of funds for particular purposes to allow technology transfers which will benefit state and local economic activity.

Accountability is required through an annual report from the agencies and laboratories to be given directly to the U. S. Congress. Cooperative research and development agreements are authorized under Sec. 3710, wherein every federal agency may enter into agreements with any entity or person to license IP innovations and technology researched and/or developed in any government-owned or government-funded facility. The enumerated authority includes the licensing of patents or any IP rights in any invention owned or financed by the government to enable the licensee to make, sell or use the inventions worldwide. In addition, special consideration is to be given to small businesses which will manufacture "substantially" in the United States. While these decisions and agreements are to be made of record, it is not clear whether these proceedings are to be of public record subjecting them to relevant "sunshine laws" which preclude closed meetings or secret proceedings.

Although Sec. 3710 (b) gives directions to implement cash award incentives to scientific, engineering and technical personnel, only those federal agencies with budgets in excess of $50 million dollars for laboratory research and development in its laboratories are subject to this directive.

D. Shared Research And Development, Financing, And Royalties

Regardless of the funding levels for the development of inventions, Sec. 3710 (c) requires that the actual inventor receive at least 15% of all the income, including royalties realized by the agency from the license or assignment of the invention. In the case of co-inventors, the designated minimum of 15% is to be equally shared by the co-inventors.

This percentage of income to the inventor is to continue even though the inventor leaves the laboratory or agency. The annual income is not to exceed $100,000 for the inventor(s), unless there is a special presidential award. Under Secs. 3710 (c) and (d), it is the President's prerogative to increase these amounts and to periodically present a Science and Technology Medal for outstanding contributions to the "promotion of technology . . . for the improvement of the economic, environmental, or social well-being of the United States."

While many large companies have facilities, personnel, and the financial resources to fund research and development, most smaller companies do not. Consequently, these smaller companies must develop funding strategies to access external resources for innovative projects. Typically, from a small pool of money funded from internal company sources, the rudimentary beginnings of a promising innovation can be generated. This, in turn, can enable a small company to apply for a federally-funded program, such as a National Institute of Health (NIH) grant. They can continue the work under seed money of $50,000 in Phase I and up to $500,000 over two years in Phase II. For example, a large, resource-rich biotechnology company such as TSI Genetics funded its initial research and development to produce human growth hormones from transgenic mice with an initial $50,000; $40,000 to produce genetically identical rabbits; $35,000 to produce human soluble CD4 in chicken eggs; and $49,000 to show technical feasibility for cryopreservation of transgenic embryos, all under separate NIH Phase I grants. These became the financial basis for a company which now has over $500 million dollars in assets. From an NIH funding base, a company can then parlay its assets by strategic corporate alliances wherein well-funded corporations are more willing to collaborate and/or invest in technology-based companies when their innovations are technically feasible. The progression can be shown in the following graph:

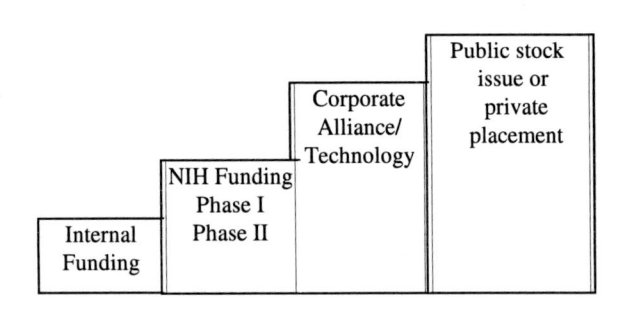

Steps in seeking research and development (R & D) funding

This kind of strategic building agenda is particularly important since there is low probability for even meritorious technologies to obtain adequate funding from outside sources without the "primitive accumulation" of some tangible threshold research and development work and a showing of "sweat equity," plus actual cash infusion into a project. Even with a basic infusion of research and development, feasibility studies, market research, and very complete presentation proposals, the statistics indicate that approximately one in 175 are able to obtain suitable funding from a major corporation. This translates to a .0057 probability for startup technology-based companies to succeed without a substantial investment of capital, research and development already in place and, in some cases, acquisition of ancillary technologies and/or a related production and distribution company. Genzyme Company, for instance, acquired a small diagnostic-based company, a specialty chemical manufacturing firm and rights to a lymphokine product line to attract necessary large scale financing for its "product line" company. Sources of major funding from risk-adverse corporations, foundations and venture capital companies are becoming increasingly bottom-line oriented, demanding fast return on investment (ROI) time frames. More projects are chasing fewer dollars. It has become increasingly urgent for startup companies to address the realities of transforming innovations into commercially successful businesses.

VII. Prepatent Considerations For Research And Development

A. Documentation of Invention

The conception and reduction to practice dates are important if the inventor files a patent application and subsequently finds that another inventor has also filed a similar application at the same time. Under these circumstances, it may be necessary for the PTO to initiate an interference proceeding, as discussed earlier, to determine the first inventor. Therefore, it is important that the inventor document prepatent actions and be able to prove both the date of "invention conception" and "reduction to practice." In the course of research and development, conception typically can be documented with the use of a bound lab book or notes which are successively numbered. The inventor should date these pages and have them witnessed by an adult who is not a family member. For the inventor who does not use a lab book, all that is necessary is that notes or sheets be dated and witnessed. A working prototype should be photographed and described, and both the photographs and written description should be dated and witnessed. A video can be used and is legally acceptable as documentation.

B. Constructive Reduction To Practice

It is usually possible to write notes about an invention; it is not always possible to reduce the invention to practice by building an operating prototype because of costs and time constraints involved. Under these circumstances, reduction to practice can be accomplished "constructively" by filing a patent application as discussed previously, unless the inventor is claiming an invention of a perpetual motion machine.

C. Interference Practice

If an invention is conceived without reducing it to practice, then a patent application should be filed; if the invention is to be reduced to practice, it should be done diligently, soon after conception. This is because of the rules relating to "interference practice." As discussed earlier, if Inventor A is involved in an interference and found to be the first to conceive the invention but the last to reduce it to practice, Inventor A could still win if diligence is shown in reducing it to practice after the date of conception.

Apart from the issue of interference, even if the invention is conceived and reduced to practice, it must not be put on the "back shelf" with the idea of working on it later. If this occurs, and Inventor A later resurrects the invention after Inventor B has received a patent, this fact will not invalidate the patent issued to Inventor B, even though Inventor A was the first to invent.

D. Meeting With A Patent Attorney

Soon after the conception and/or reduction to practice of the invention, the inventor should meet with a patent attorney, many of whom will give a free first consultation which usually lasts from a half hour to an hour. Expected fees need to be discussed and costs of the patent process should be addressed at this time.

E. Disclosing Information To An Attorney

If the inventor is to ask the attorney for some general cost ranges in doing certain patent work during the meeting, it may be necessary to give more detailed information about the invention so that a more accurate estimate can be given. Some inventors are apprehensive or even refuse to discuss the invention with legal counsel fearing that the invention might be stolen. This is an understandable concern but, in order to determine whether the patent attorney is technically qualified to handle the invention, generally it is necessary to describe the subject matter. It should be indicated, however, that the attorney-client relationship imposes a fiduciary duty on the part of the attorney to keep disclosures of patentable information in strict confidence. Failure on the part of a patent attorney to safeguard such disclosures would be a breach of the professional code of ethics and could result in legal sanctions and penalties.

F. Avoiding A Conflict of Interest

While the precise features of the invention do not have to be discussed during the initial interview with an attorney, sufficient details should be given for another salient reason. It is possible that the attorney has another client working on the same invention, or one similar thereto. There may be a potential conflict of interest between clients. For example, assume that the inventor has invented a particular feature for a computer disk drive. It may not be enough merely to tell the attorney that the invention relates to an electromechanical device since that attorney may also be representing another client in that field of invention.

G. Preparation for Meeting With A Patent Attorney

Apart from an initial visit, a patent attorney normally charges by the hour rather than by the task, although an estimate of the costs involved for particular tasks can be requested. Therefore, it is important to use the conference time efficiently. As a result, after selecting the patent attorney and before the conference, the inventor should prepare the presentation in detail. Most important, the inventor should have a detailed written description of the invention, with drawings or sketches complete with numerical cross references between the description and drawings. The written description should include:

1. details of the particular invention
2. what has been done in the prior art, if known,
3. how the invention differs from what was done in the prior art, and

4. the advantages of the invention resulting from these differences. If the invention is the previously described computer disk drive, the inventor should also describe other related devices, the differences between them and the advantages of the invention.

In addition to this information, the inventor should be prepared to tell the attorney who the co-inventors are, if the inventor is not the only or sole inventor, or if the inventor is not sure, be prepared to tell the facts which led to the invention. If the inventor is working for a company in a related field or has previously worked for a company in a related field, an explanation should be made as to how the invention came about; and the invention should be compared to the work done for the current employer or past employer. Some employers demand rights to all inventions of their employees. Finally, the attorney will give directions as to how the inventor might proceed with the invention. The inventor should consider the following questions: Is the inventor planning to manufacture and market the product?

Or, would the inventor rather have another small or large company manufacture and market under a license agreement?

H. Prepatent Options Available

Once the inventor selects and meets with a patent attorney and describes the invention along with the background of the invention, several options are available.

1. <u>Preliminary Patentability Search</u>

A preliminary patentability search can be performed to determine the first inventor. During the search, an attempt is made to find an earlier patent or publication which describes the invention and which would then prevent the issuance of a patent for the same invention. There are several ways the search can be effected. If a patent attorney has the search performed, an associate in Washington, D.C., who searches for prior art patents in the PTO public search room may be engaged. Most large universities have a Class A government depository where a patent search can be done. This search will be far more time-consuming since most Class A government depositories do not separate the patents into classes and subclasses but only into classes.

Therefore, rather than searching a subclass for all types of computer disk drives, specifically, the inventor of a new disk drive may have to search an entire general class which includes all computers. Nevertheless, if an inventor has the time and/or ability, it could be less costly to attempt a preliminary search. Another possibility is to conduct a search on a computer database, such as Dialog or Lexis.

Whether the inventor has the patent attorney conduct a search in Washington, D.C., or it is done by the inventor on a database, in a government depository or in the public search room in Washington, D.C., such a patent search does not guarantee that all of the relevant prior art has been located. A professional search made in the PTO in Washington, D.C., will likely uncover most of the pertinent art. However, it is possible that a prior article or publication other than a patent exists. A typical preliminary patentability search conducted in Washington, D.C., does not generally take into account publications other than patents and, unless a relatively large amount of money is spent on the search, it will not include most foreign patents. Although unlikely, it is possible that a particular patent may not be in the files at the time the search is made because another searcher has pulled it from the shelf.

2. <u>Right-to-Use or Infringement Search</u>

A preliminary patentability search should be distinguished from a "right-to-use" or "infringement search." The preliminary patentability search merely gives an indication of the likelihood of obtaining a patent for the invention. It does not necessarily disclose all patents which might be infringed upon should a product embodying the invention be produced. Consider the following example which will clarify this concept. The inventor has invented a computer disk drive and a preliminary patentability search is conducted which discloses a drive that uses both a magnetic storage feature and a laser storage feature. But the subject invention uses only a laser feature and that is the subject of the invention claims. The claims in the prior art patents may specifically recite both the magnetic and the laser claims. From this set of facts, the patent attorney would conclude that a patent could not be obtained on the invention since it has already been disclosed in a patent. However, this patent would not preclude making the invention since the invention does not include a magnetic element which is required by the claims in the prior patent.

In the last example, consider that a preliminary patentability search was conducted but did not include a right-to-use or infringement search. The searcher was only concerned with finding a prior art disclosure of the computer disk drive in question, not necessarily a prior patent having a broad enough claim to protect the invention. It is more difficult and time-consuming to review all the possible claims covered in patents and their disclosures. Therefore, the search could easily have omitted a patent which shows a magnetic drive since that patent would not preclude the patenting of a laser drive. However, had the searcher been required to conduct a right-to-use or infringement search, the claims would need to be reviewed not only in the magnetic and laser patent found during the search but also in the patents which include all computer disk drives. Also, this search may have disclosed claims broad enough to preclude a patent for a laser drive invention.

A patent attorney may not suggest a right-to-use or infringement search at the beginning of the patent process. However, if the invention requires a large capital investment, either by the inventor or investors in collaboration with a company or venture capitalists, this may be a wise business decision, sometimes required by those contributing the capital.

3. <u>Filing Without a Search</u>

Another option is to file a patent application without a search. This may be necessary because of time constraints. For example, if the inventor has already been selling the invention for almost a year, or if it were published almost a year ago, the inventor may not have time to do a search before the one-year statutory period expires. Another reason to forego a search is that the inventor may be confident that there is no relevant prior art because of familiarity in the field to which the invention applies. Still another reason not to do a search is that the inventor may plan to market the invention whether or not a patent is granted and/or the inventor recognizes the advantage in utilizing the patent pending notice for a period of time.

4. <u>Waiting to Search or File</u>

The inventor may end the visit with a patent attorney without authorizing either a search or the preparation of a patent application. A decision may be made to do further work either in developing the invention or in building an actual prototype. This is typically the case when the invention is only a product concept and general in scope. It may be that further development will result in a modification of the invention or even change entirely what the inventor originally had conceived the invention to be.

5. <u>Seeking Financial Backing</u>

Another reason for waiting to file a patent application is to seek initial financial backing. This may be in the form of an outside submission made by the inventor to a company or to a venture capitalist. In either case, in order for an evaluation to be made, it will be necessary to make a disclosure of the invention.

I. Confidential/Nonconfidential Disclosures

Many companies will not accept an invention disclosure without the inventor agreeing to execute a nonconfidential agreement. This type of agreement typically states that the inventor agrees to disclose the invention on a "nonconfidential" basis and rely only on the patent laws to protect the inventor's interests. The reasons for this policy include the company's position that at the time it receives the outside submission from an inventor, a research group within the same company may be doing research in a similar area. A company does not want to be legally bound to a confidential disclosure agreement with the inventor, since at the same time, the company may already be doing research similar to the newly submitted invention. By providing a nonconfidential agreement which relies solely on the patent laws, the company does not risk losing rights obtained from its own research and development.

If the inventor plans to seek financial backing from a company, especially a large company, the inventor may be requested to sign a nonconfidential agreement. The alternative is to negotiate an agreement with an outside company by signing a confidential disclosure agreement, wherein the invention will be kept secret for a certain period of time.

Before disclosing the invention to third parties, it is important that the invention be well-documented. However, whether the invention is simple or complex, the inventor is at risk when disclosing to any third party the details without either a confidential disclosure agreement and/or having filed a patent application.

Disclosure via nonconfidential or confidential disclosure agreements present real risks to the inventor. While there is no sovereign talisman to totally protect the inventor from the perils of disclosure, the inventor must be aware that companies great and small may simply appropriate part or all of the disclosed invention and proceed to commercialize it. Some companies may decide to "design around" the disclosed invention and may do so with impunity. In either case, a company can place the considerable and expensive burden of defense on the inventor who may not be able to sustain effective litigation against a company with a larger "war chest."

There are many cases illustrating the clear and present dangers of disclosures to seemingly "reputable" companies. There are also cases wherein an inventor took the risk of disclosure, had the invention stolen but persisted in litigation with a final judgment favoring the inventor. For instance, Robert Kearns disclosed his intermittent wiper blade device and displayed a working prototype to the Ford Motor Company, which declined to license the device, but began to manufacture and sell it. Kearns litigated for over ten years, had two nervous breakdowns, and was impoverished until he won a $14.5 million dollar award in 1991 and is currently suing other automobile manufacturers worldwide. In 1997, Ronald Chasteen won a $57 million dollar judgment against Polaris Industries for illegally appropriating his invention for a fuel injection system for snowmobiles. This award came after litigating for nine years.

J. Initial Marketing

An inventor may elect to file the patent application as soon as possible and, if seeking financial backing, test market the invention immediately to determine how successful it might be. The United States Patent Act allows the inventor one year to exploit the invention before a patent application needs to be filed. Therefore, if the invention has been carefully documented as described above, the inventor may want to determine how successful the invention might be before making a decision to spend money on patent protection. If the inventor determines that the invention will probably be a commercial failure, the inventor may not want to go further. If the invention would likely be successful in the marketplace, the inventor may want to try to obtain patent protection. However, if the inventor chooses this approach, the inventor will lose rights to file corresponding applications in certain foreign countries, as will be discussed later.

K. Maintaining Invention As A Trade Secret

The inventor may opt not to do a search, file an application or take the various steps already discussed but rather may elect to protect the invention as a trade secret while, at the same time, commercializing it. Obviously, if the inventor opts for trade secret protection, it must be the type of invention which cannot be "discovered" after commercialization.

The advantage of keeping the invention a trade secret is that the inventor can retain a monopoly for more than the 14 or 20-year period of patent protection. On the other hand, one takes the chance that someone else will subsequently discover the "secret" of the invention independently, by a security leak, or by industrial espionage.

It is not necessary that the inventor decide immediately whether or not to keep the invention secret. The inventor can still proceed with a patent application to see what kind of patent protection can be received. It may be determined that either a patent with relatively broad claims or a very limited patent can be obtained or, in fact, that no patent can be issued. The inventor also has the option to abandon the patent application, however, the PTO is required to keep the application secret even if it is abandoned. But if the patent application is abandoned, the invention could still be protected as a trade secret. The Uniform Trade Secrets Act (UTSA) Sec. 1(4) (1985) provides a working definition for trade secrets:

> Trade secret means information, including formula, pattern, compilation, program device, method, technique or protective process that:
>
> > (i) derives independent economic value, actual or potential from not being generally known, and not being readily ascertainable by proper means by other persons who can obtain economic value from its disclosure or use, and
> >
> > (ii) is the subject of efforts that are reasonable under the circumstances to maintain secrecy.

While some courts have had some difficulty in defining a trade secret in such a succinct manner, most courts recognize it as a matter to be decided by the trier of fact, be it a judge or jury. There have been many trade secrets held to be protected in the broad areas of chemical compounds, business knowledge about customer lists and buyer motivation, or complex circuitry and software programs.

While many trade secrets relate to compounds containing secret ingredients, various trade secrets involve processes or methods of processing information or combinations thereof, as well as use of special ingredients. If a composition of ingredients can be chemically analyzed and reverse-engineered and, thereby be reproduced, it is no longer a protectable trade secret. However, most trade secrets of composition products are a combination of ingredients combined in certain quantities by specific processes. Coca Cola is a well-known commercial beverage which was invented in 1895 by a pharmacist, but the beverage was not patented. It has been protected as a trade secret for over a century. Despite the fact that the syrup component can be chemically analyzed and reverse-engineered, other elements such as quantities, procedures and processes are combined together to produce a commercially successful product based on a well-guarded trade secret.

As may be surmised, theft of trade secrets can occur in several ways, including disclosure of trade secrets to competitive companies by employees or ex-employees of the companies holding the trade secrets. In one case which resulted in an award of $1.2 million dollars in damages and $250,000 in legal fees, a competitive company hired away 80% of management and the skilled work force of a company holding trade secrets. These key personnel in the aggregate brought all relevant trade secrets with them and assisted in making and selling a product protected by the UTSA. See *C. Albert Sauter Co. v. R. S. Sauter Co.*, 368 F.Supp. 501 (1973). In 1997, General Electric and Dow Chemical settled a lawsuit involving violation of Dow's trade secrets by "enticing" and/or "recruitment" of at least 14 former Dow key employees. Part of the court order barred General Electric from placing a former Dow key employee in a company position where the Dow trade secrets could be used. It is well-settled in the area of trade secret litigation that failure on the part of a company to establish a trade secret program and supervise employee activities privy to trade secrets will result in a loss of trade secret protection from the courts.

VIII. Licensing Or Sale Of The Invention

A. Types of Licenses

An inventor may elect to produce and market an invention; an alternative is to grant a license for the invention to others. There are several different types of licensing structures from which to choose. The most desirable type assumes that the inventor has a patent to license but is without the manufacturing and production resources and/or "know-how." On that assumption, there are two essential types of licensing agreements: a nonexclusive license or an exclusive license.

1. Nonexclusive License

With a "nonexclusive patent license," the licensee is given certain rights under the patent, while at the same time, the licensor may license the same rights to additional licensees under the same patent. For example, the inventor may wish to license with companies A, B, and D the right to manufacture and sell the invention. The inventor may also wish to retain the right to do so.

Normally, a nonexclusive patent license of this type requires a royalty payment to be paid by the licensee to the licensor, *e.g.*, the patent owner or assignor, based on the sales of the product or products incorporating the invention. Since this agreement is nonexclusive, it may require a smaller fee or royalty than an exclusive license and the terms and conditions are incorporated into the agreement.

2. <u>Exclusive License</u>

The exclusive patent agreement allows the licensee exclusive rights under the patent to make and sell the invention. In the case of an exclusive license, a larger minimum royalty payment and a larger license fee should be expected. Since the licensee is the only one who has the rights to make and sell products embodying the invention under the license agreement, the licensor should be protected by minimum royalties and a front-end fee, which will secure the licensor's interests, whether or not the licensee does as well as expected. If there is an annual minimum fee of $25,000 and, in a particular year, the earned royalties, *e.g.*, those based on actual sales by the licensee do not amount to the minimum royalty of $25,000, the licensee must nevertheless supplement the earned royalties to make up the difference to keep the license in full force and effect. This ensures that the licensee will use "best efforts" to sell at least enough of the product to meet the minimum royalties.

B. Royalty Payments And License Fee Basis

The amounts paid for the initial license fee and subsequent payments of royalties will generally depend upon the subject matter involved, as well as motivation, profit potential, and assets expended by the licensor, capital investment of the licensee, and the negotiating positions of both parties. In some cases, royalty payments of 20% of gross sales revenues are possible, while in others a royalty payment of 1% may be considered reasonable. However, the licensor must be careful of the language used to define the basis for calculating the percentage of royalty payments.

Twenty percent of "net profit" may be zero dollars or even a negative royalty since that basis would allow the licensee company to deduct corporate expenses if the agreement is without any accounting controls to protect the licensor. A licensor may be put unwittingly in a position to subsidize a lavish corporate lifestyle for the licensee company which could, with impunity, include corporate jet airplanes and villas in the south of France to which the licensor may not be an invited guest.

A well-defined basis for calculating royalty payments would make 6% of "gross sales revenues" much more equitable and easier to monitor than 20% of "net profits." While it is well-established in the law and in standard accounting practice that proprietary rights are intangible assets, there is no litmus paper test for the determination of a reasonable initial license fee to be paid to the licensor. The same considerations for negotiating a royalty amount apply to the license fee as well. However, most experienced negotiators accept reasonable "trade-offs" in arriving at the license fee such as the maturity of the invention, market need, competition, costs of tooling and molds, and start-up expenses to produce and distribute the invention. Within the context of these variables, a common ground usually can be found based on the total time, costs and "sweat equity" expended by the licensor which should be recouped with the initial license fee.

In order to further protect the licensor, a typical exclusive license may require that the licensee use its best efforts to market the product and should contain a noncompete clause. This prevents a licensee from tying up the invention through an exclusive arrangement and allowing it to languish. Without these clauses, a licensee could even promote a competitive product, thereby suppressing the invention to the detriment of the licensor.

C. Sale Of A Patent

An alternative to an exclusive or nonexclusive license agreement is an outright sale of the patent. There is little apparent difference between an exclusive patent license and an outright sale if the exclusive patent license is for the full term of the patent and covers all fields of use without territorial restrictions. All the considerations applicable to a license agreement apply also to an outright sale of a patent. However, in the case of an outright sale, the seller runs the risk of the buyer filing under the bankruptcy code with the result of having the patent or invention considered to be an asset of the buyer and therefore subject to creditors. This is of great concern to the seller, if the sale involves annual payments over the life of the patent and the full purchase price is not received at the time of sale.

Whether the license or sale agreement is a less complex patent agreement or a much more sophisticated "proprietary rights" agreement which may include patents, know-how, trade secrets, trademarks, copyrights and service marks, it is advisable to use competent legal, technical and financial counsel in drafting the agreements and as a resource in negotiations. At the same time, it is important that the licensor also participate in the negotiation and transaction process. If the transaction is complex and multifaceted, it may be necessary to bring in a team which has expertise in relevant technology, proprietary rights, accounting, tax law, and business contracts.

IX. Filing For Foreign Patents

A. Time Restrictions

If the inventor's U. S. patent application was filed before being commercialized or published, even if the patent has not been issued, the inventor may file a corresponding application in most countries throughout the world. However, the foreign application must be filed within one year of the U. S. Patent application filing date. The inventor may still file corresponding foreign applications in most foreign countries after one year from the U. S. filing date but the benefit of the filing date of the United States application would not be received. If foreign applications are filed more than a year after the invention has been published, patent rights will be lost in those countries which have "an absolute novelty law," as discussed below.

B. Foreign Patent Applications

1. <u>National Patent Applications</u>

There are three different ways to file foreign patent applications. The first way is to file an individual application in each country. These are often referred to as "national" applications. Each country then examines its own application according to its procedures and patent laws.

2. **European Patent Convention**

A second way is to file a European Patent Convention (EPC) application. This type of application covers a large number of countries in Europe. Generally, when the inventor is interested in filing in five or more countries, it is more economical to file an EPC application instead of individual national applications.

3. **Patent Cooperation Treaty Application**

This is actually a filing procedure and does not result in a complete or substantive application, however, it does provide more time to decide whether or not national applications are desired. The PCT application designates a number of member countries and includes most of the European, Oriental and North American countries. Within 20 months from the filing date of the PCT application or the priority date of the U. S. application, the inventor must convert the PCT application to one or more national applications based on the claims of the invention which were originally designated in the PCT application. An extension of 10 months beyond the original 20 months is possible under a PCT proceeding known as "Chapter II." The costs involved in filing individual national applications after filing the PCT application are the same as they would have been had the PCT application not been filed.

As indicated above, the United States can be designated in a PCT application and it is possible to file the PCT application or a foreign application before a U. S. patent application is filed. However, in both cases, it is necessary to obtain a clearance from the U. S. Department of Commerce before filing a PCT or other foreign U. S. patent applications. With regard to PCT applications, the Patent Cooperation Treaty office automatically notifies the U. S. Department of Commerce upon receipt of the application filed by the U. S. applicant. If a United States application is filed, clearance is not needed from the Department of Commerce to file corresponding foreign applications if the foreign applications are filed within 6 months following the filing date of the United States application.

C. Absolute Novelty Requirements

Most European countries and Japan have "absolute novelty" requirements. This law may differ somewhat from country to country. Most of these countries' laws state that a patent cannot be obtained if it has been published elsewhere or is publicly available or commercialized in any European country or other country, such as Japan, before the effective filing date of the application in that country. Taiwan also has an absolute novelty requirement and it does not have any reciprocating treaty or international agreement with the United States. Therefore, a Taiwanese application is not relevant to a U.S. filing date.

To avoid the consequences of absolute novelty laws without first filing in a foreign country which has absolute novelty laws, a patent application should be filed in the United States before publication or commercial use of the invention, and subsequently be filed in the foreign country within a year from the U.S. filing date. This assumes that the foreign country will afford the benefit of the U.S. filing date. However, if it does, the inventor is not barred from filing in that country as a result of absolute novelty, even if a publication takes place or the invention is commercialized before filing in that country. By receiving the benefit of the U. S. filing date, the absolute novelty requirements do not qualify or limit the inventor's right to patent protection in those countries which have absolute novelty requirements.

"We might find ourselves at the mercy of Luddites who did not want to take a chance on any form of change."
– James Watson, Nobel Laureate

X. Conclusion: A Response To Change

The technology innovation research and development process can become complex very quickly; even seemingly simple devices when designed, reduced to practice, tested, patented and commercialized may take on lives of their own. They can then threaten to take over the lives of their makers. Adam Smith in his classic *Wealth of Nations*, published in the auspicious year of 1776, provides a clear view of the technological, economic and business realities of developing, producing and selling a straight pin. While a straight pin appears to be simple, it is not simple when reduced from mind to matter and transmogrified into money by the machinations of the marketplace. His "invisible hand," Smith's symbol for the forces of an unfettered market, holds a scepter which rules us all. With the visible hand of the government now at work in the marketplace, the centers of power become less clear, the lines between the rulers and ruled become blurred, and ways of making money from products become increasingly problematic.

There are lessons to be learned from both crushing failures and great triumphs. One is the lesson which instructs us to touch *terra firma*, even when exploring *terra incognita* in the uncharted regions of science and technology. Maps and compasses need to be consulted on a regular basis lest inventors becomes hopelessly lost. It should also be learned that attempts to defy the laws of "financial gravity" in these endeavors, albeit bold and noble, will result in a jolting and unceremonious crash. This will lead to a swift and certain demise of a project, personnel and the business entity. Risk management assessments, adequate budgeting and realistic expectations of a technology project contribute to a successful outcome. Reality checks need to be made regularly and always before a check is written. Inadequate project financing or lack of budget controls are examples of

Charles Dickens' "formula for misery," which is: "Income, twenty pounds; expenditures, twenty pounds six pence."

Approximately one hundred years after the PTO was opened in 1790, it was closed for over a year because it was thought that almost everything worthwhile had been invented; however, an astonishing array of technologies has been patented since it reopened for business. In fact, the world, its environment and all living things have been profoundly transformed by new technologies in the past century. A cerebral, emotional and technological Rubicon has been crossed; it is not certain how many bridges have been left standing for a retreat, if necessary. In this crossing, IP rights in the form of patented technologies and those protected as trade secrets have provided the claimed and guarded territory enforced by the coercive powers of the government. The rest of commercialized science and technology has been hewn from the forests of the marketplace, sometimes graphically referred to as a jungle. Innovations, in this primal arena, whether protected IP or not, thrive, survive, languish or die. IP augments the probability of technological survival in the stream, river or swamp of commerce but it does not guarantee its commercial success.

Moreover, IP needs to be understood and properly implemented with assistance from those with expertise in the various related specialty disciplines, working with scientists, technicians, technology managers, company directors and inventors.

While the perennial desire to transmute base metal into gold in the business of technology innovation is still strong, especially because of the multiplicity of demands worldwide, magical alchemy is still not available. The science and technology innovation landscape is littered with litigation, errors and the travail that goes with them. On the same landscape, scientific and technological castles, cathedrals and fortresses have been constructed and display unimaginable financial successes, achievements and benefits for large numbers of citizens.

Charles Darwin may have inspired Charles Spencer's "social Darwinism" with its "survival of the fittest" refrain which has evolved from a term of art to mean that those who are to survive in the primordial jungle must be the most powerful, the strongest and, perhaps, the most ruthless. When this is added to the contemporary application of Machiavellian precepts, "treachery" may also be added to the recommended business survival kit. However, a close look at Darwin's own seminal work, *The Origin of Species,* discloses that he understood the "fittest" to mean not the most powerful, not the strongest, not the most ruthless, nor the most treacherous, but those most responsive to change. In any type of competitive environment, including technology innovation, the tools and strategies most helpful are those which assist people and institutions to be the most responsive to change. These changes may be slowly evolutionary or devolutionary; they may be rapid in both directions of the learning curve followed by the species and the institutions they create. Where there are rapid changes occurring, education and training are needed to keep apace in order to manage them and to derive maximum benefit from them. With traditional educational institutions groaning under the collective weight of numbers – increased numbers of students, decreasing number of dollars available, steadily declining national test scores and an "inflation of honors" in terms of bloated GPA numbers – improved methods are required in both traditional educational systems and in corporate training departments. Without accelerated improvements and higher standards in both areas of education and training, it is unlikely that the enormous economic potential of technology innovations can be realized.

Collaborations among traditional schools, private companies and governmental agencies are critical to the development and commercialization of innovative technologies. These collaborations can include cooperative scientific and technology education programs to meet a multiplicity of objectives. The establishment of IP and technology transfer departments in colleges and universities is becoming a major source of revenues for future generations as budget cuts for higher education increase. If we are properly prepared in these ways, change can mean opportunity, not crisis. Change can be embraced by all those wanting to build a technologically enhanced society which is successful and which benefits from its decisive responses to change.

Appendix

- Endnotes..A-1

- Bibliography, Table of Cases, and Authorities..........B-1

- U.S. Patent & Trademark Office Fee Schedule.........C-1

- Process and Methods Patent...............................D-1

- Mechanical and Material Patent..........................E-1

- Biotechnology and Methods Patent......................F-1

- Design Patent...G-1

- License or Sale Checklist................................H-1

Endnotes

1. *History of Thoracic Surgery - From Early Times*, ed. Raymond Hart, 1996.

2. Anticipation includes: 1) prior patent 2) publication 3) use 4) knowledge or 5) known inventions.

3. Doctrine of Equivalents comment: The *Pennwalt* case (1987) begins a judicial trend toward the easier designing around of issued patents with impunity. This trend erodes the doctrine of equivalents which had worked to preserve patentees' protection against potential infringers and to prevent infringement of an issued patent. Prior to *Pennwalt*, if means and function of an alleged infringement were shown to be essentially "equivalent" to elements of an issued patent, there was a presumption that infringement occurred.

The precedential *Pennwalt* case reaches its apogee in an unpublished opinion by a panel of the court wherein the panel attempts to articulate its view of means plus function. It states that there is no infringement even though the means clause is identical to the accused element and that the element is interchangeable with the element in the patent specification supporting the means clause. This is because the (two) elements are not "structural equivalents" even though this interchangeability demonstrates them to be

A-1

"equivalent structures." Baltimore Therapeutic v. Loredan Medical cited as a reference.

The use of the language appears to further erode the doctrine of equivalents; changing the order of the words, "equivalent" and "structure(al)" does not seem to substantiate the argument but rather suggests a way to modify the doctrine of equivalents. In fact, the court in Baltimore Therapeutics considered interchangeability of components as "irrelevant" to substantial equivalence.

However, in *Hilton Davis Chemical v. Warner Jenkinson* (1995), the court suggested that interchangeability of elements is "potent evidence" of substantial similarity, hence, equivalence. This holding recognizes the potential viability of the doctrine of equivalents as relevant to the issue of designing around an issued patent. However, its continued viability remains uncertain since Hilton Davis Chemical has been granted a writ of certiorari by the United States Supreme Court.

Bibliography

Articles

Abramowitz, Moses, "Resources and Output Trends in the United States Since 1870," *American Economics Review* (May 1956).

Brinton, Joyce, "University Perspective," AIPLA Quarterly Journal 16 no. 3 & 4 (1989).

Drucker, Peter, "The Rise of the Knowledge Society," *Wilson Quarterly* (Spring 1993).

Ermene, James, "Interview With Chester Carlson," *Dartmouth Press* (December 1965).

Fineberg, Harvey, "Irresistible Medical Technologies: Weighing the Costs and Benefits," *Technology Review* (November-December 1984).

Friedman, David, "A Policy That Punishes American Ingenuity," *IPC* (November 1995).

Hallwin, Andrew, "Patenting the Results of Genetic Engineering Research: An Overview," *Banbury Report* (1982).

Hanan, Michael, "Corporate Growth Through Venture Management," *Harvard Business Review* (January-February 1969).

"New Development in Biotechnology: Patenting Life–Special Report–OTA–BA-370," *U. S. Government Printing Office* (1989).

Pressman, David, "Government Hits Inventors With Double Whammy But You Can Fight For Restoration of 17-Year Term," *IPC* (November 1995).

Quinn, James Brian, "Technological Innovation, Entrepreneurship and Strategy," *Sloan Management Review* (1979).

Tauber, Edward, "How Market Research Discourages Major Innovation," *Business Horizons, University of Indiana Press* (1970),

Books

Conlin, David and Gregory Williams. *Biotechnology Patent Practice.* Patent Resources Group, 1995.

Cox, Archibald. *The Court and the Constitution.* Houghton Mifflin Co., 1987.

Dampier, William Cecil. *History of Science.* Cambridge University Press, 1966.

Darwin, Charles. *The Origin of Species.* Collier Publications, 1961.

Hart, Raymond. Ed. *History of Thoracic Surgery – From Early Times.* C. C. Thomas, 1996.

Hobbes, Thomas. *Leviathan.* Oxford University Press, 1982.

Kenney, Michael. *Biotechnology: The University-Industrial Complex.* Yale University Press, 1986.

Kuhn, Thomas. *The Structure of Scientific Revolution.* Harvard University Press, 1963.

Long, Pamela. Ed. *Science and Technology in Medieval Society.* New York Academy of Science, 1985.

McConnell, Terrance. *Moral Issues in Health Care.* Wadsworth Publishing Co., 1997.

Ono, R. Dana. *The Business of Biotechnology: From the Bench to the Street.* Butterworth-Heinemann, 1991.

Samuels, Jeffrey. Ed. *Patent, Trademark and Copyright Laws.* The Bureau of National Affairs, 1989.

Schnookler, Jacob. *Inventions and Economic Growth.* Harvard University Press, 1966.

Sigerist, Henry. *Making Medical History.* Johns Hopkins University Press, 1997.

Smith, Adam. *Wealth of Nations.* Modern Library Press, 1937.

Volti, Rudi. *Society and Technological Change.* St. Martin's Press, 1988.

Cases

Brenner v. Manson, 86 S. Ct. 1033 (1966)......33

C. Albert Sauter Co. v. R. S. Sauter Co., 368 F.Supp. 501 (1973......96

Cochran Consulting, Inc. v. Uwatec USA, Inc., 96-1145 (1996)......50

Corning Glass Works v. Sumitomo Elec., 868 F2d 1257 (1989)......54

Cuno Corp. v. Automatic Devices Corp., 315 U.S. 84 (1941)......33

Diamond v. Chakrabarty, 447 U.S. 303 (1980)......46

Golgaber ex parte 11/8/96, PTO Appeal N. 95-2038 (1995)......34

Graham v. John Deere Co., 383 U.S.1 (1966)......35

Graver Tank Mfg. Co., Inc. v. Linde Air Products Co., 339 U.S. 605 (1950)........55

London v. Carson Ririe Scott & Co., 946 F2d (1991)......................................55

MacPherson v. Buick Motor Co., 217 N.Y. 382 (1916)...2

Pennwalt Corp. v. Durand-Wayland, Inc., 833 F2d 931 (1987)..........................54

Pfizer Medical Inc. Pfizer Inc. v. Int'll Rectifier Corp., 586 C.D. Cal. (1985)....50

Sarkisian v. Winn-Proof Corp., 606 F2d, 671 (1982)...34

Schwinn Bicycle Co. v. Goodyear Tire & Rubber Co., 444 F2d 295 (1970)..........45

Smith Int'l, Inc. v. Hughes Tool Co., 81 C.D.Cal. (1986)...............................50

W.R. Grace & Co. v. Western U.S. Industries, Inc., 608 F2d (9th Cir. 1979)...40

Authorities

Code of Federal Regulations, Food & Drug Administration, (1993).

U. S. Patent and Trademark Office
Fee Schedule effective October 1, 1996

Fee Code	37CFR	Description	Fee	Small Entity if applic
Patent Filing Fees				
101/201	1.16(a)	Basic filing fee - utility	770.00	385.00
102/102	1.16(b)	Independent claims in excess of three	80.00	40.00
103/203	1.16(c)	Claims in excess of twenty	22.00	11.00
104/204	1.16(d)	Multiple dependent claim	260.00	130.00
105/205	1.16(e)	Surcharge - Late filing fee or oath or declaration	130.00	65.00
106/206	1.16(f)	Design filing fee	320.00	160.00
107/207	1.16(g)	Plant filing fee 530.00	265.00	
108/208	1.16(h)	Reissue filing fee	770.00	385.00
109/209	1.16(I)	Reissue independent claims over original patent	80.00	40.00
110/210	1.16(j)	Reissue claims in excess of 20 & over original patent	22.00	11.00
114/214	1.16(k)	Provisional application filing fee	150.00	25.00
127/227	1.16(l)	Surcharge - Late provisional filing fee or cover sheet	50.00	25.00
139	1.17(k)	Non-English specification	130.00	
Patent Issue Fees				
142/242	1.18(a)	Utility issue fee 1,290.00	645.00	
143/243	1.18(b)	Design issue fee	440.00	220.00
144/244	1.18(c)	Plant issue fee 650.00	325.00	
Plant Maintenance Fees		*Application Filed on or after December 12, 1980*		
183/283	1.20(e)	Due at 3.5 years	1,020.00	510.00
184/284	1.20(f)	Due at 7.5 years	2,050.00	1,025.00
185/285	1.20(g)	Due at 11.5 years	3,080.00	1,540.00
186/286	1.20(h)	Surcharge - Late payment within 6 months	130.00	65.00
187	1.20(i)(1)	Surcharge after expiration-Late payment is unavoidable	680.00	
188	1.20(i)(2)	Surcharge after expiration-Late payment is unintentional	1,600.00	
Miscellaneous Patent Fees				
111	1.20(j)(1)	Extension of term of patent	1,090.00	
124	1.20(j)(2)	Initial application for interim extension (see 37CFR 1.790)	410.00	
125	1.20(j)(3)	Subsequent application for interim extension (see 37CFR 1.790)	210.00	
112	1.17(n)	Requesting publication of SIR - Prior to examiner's action	900.00*	
113	1.17(o)	Requesting publication of SIR - After examiner's action	1,790.00*	
146/246	1.17(r)	For filing a submission after final rejection (see 37 CFR 1.129(a)	270.00	385.00
149/249	1.17(s)	For each additional invention to be examined (see 37 CFR 1.129(b)	100.00	385.00
145	1.20(a)	Certificate of correction	100.00	
147	1.20(c)	For filing a request for reexamination	2,460.00	
148/248	1.20(d)	Statutory Disclaimer	1,110.00	55.00

*Reduced by Basic Filing Fee

United States Patent [19]

[11] Patent Number: **4,703,159**
[45] Date of Patent: **Oct. 27, 1987**

METHOD OF MANUFACTURING LIGHTWEIGHT THERMO-BARRIER MATERIAL

Inventor: Winford Blair, La Mesa, Calif.

Assignee: The United States of America as represented by the Administrator of the National Aeronautics and Space Administration, Washington, D.C.

Appl. No.: 314,667

Filed: Oct. 26, 1981

Related U.S. Application Data

Continuation-in-part of Ser. No. 165,277, Jul. 2, 1980, abandoned.

Int. Cl.^{4} B23K 1/04; B32B 3/12
U.S. Cl. 219/78.12; 219/78.02;
219/85 E; 219/85 M; 228/181; 428/593; 428/594
Field of Search .... 428/73, 178, 593, 594; 219/78.11, 78.12, 78.02, 85 E, 85 M; 228/181

[56] References Cited

U.S. PATENT DOCUMENTS

1,228,763	6/1917	Ellis	428/72
1,914,207	6/1933	Knight	428/73
2,481,046	9/1949	Scurlock	219/78.12
3,073,268	1/1963	Cole	219/78.11
3,151,712	10/1964	Jackson	428/174
4,205,118	5/1980	Schubert	219/78.12

FOREIGN PATENT DOCUMENTS

| 54-18232 | 7/1979 | Japan | 228/181 |
| 1438842 | 6/1976 | United Kingdom | 219/85 E |

Primary Examiner—B. A. Reynolds
Assistant Examiner—Alfred S. Keve
Attorney, Agent, or Firm—Robert F. Kempf; Nina M. Lawrence; John R. Manning

[57] ABSTRACT

A method of manufacturing thermal barrier structures comprising at least three dimpled cores separated by flat plate material with the outer surface of the flat plate material joined together by diffusion bonding.

11 Claims, 8 Drawing Figures

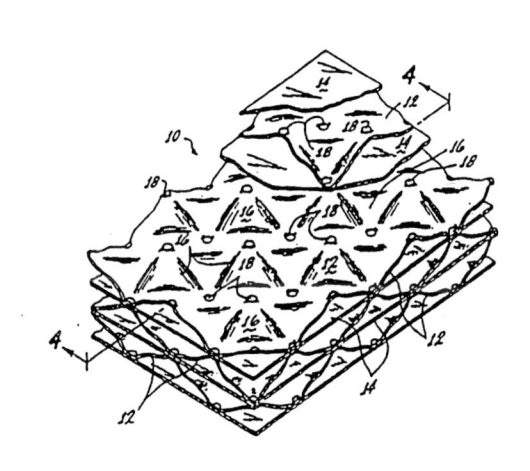

Process and Methods Patent for a mechanical, thermal barrier/heat transfer material for heat shield use.

D-1

Fig. 2

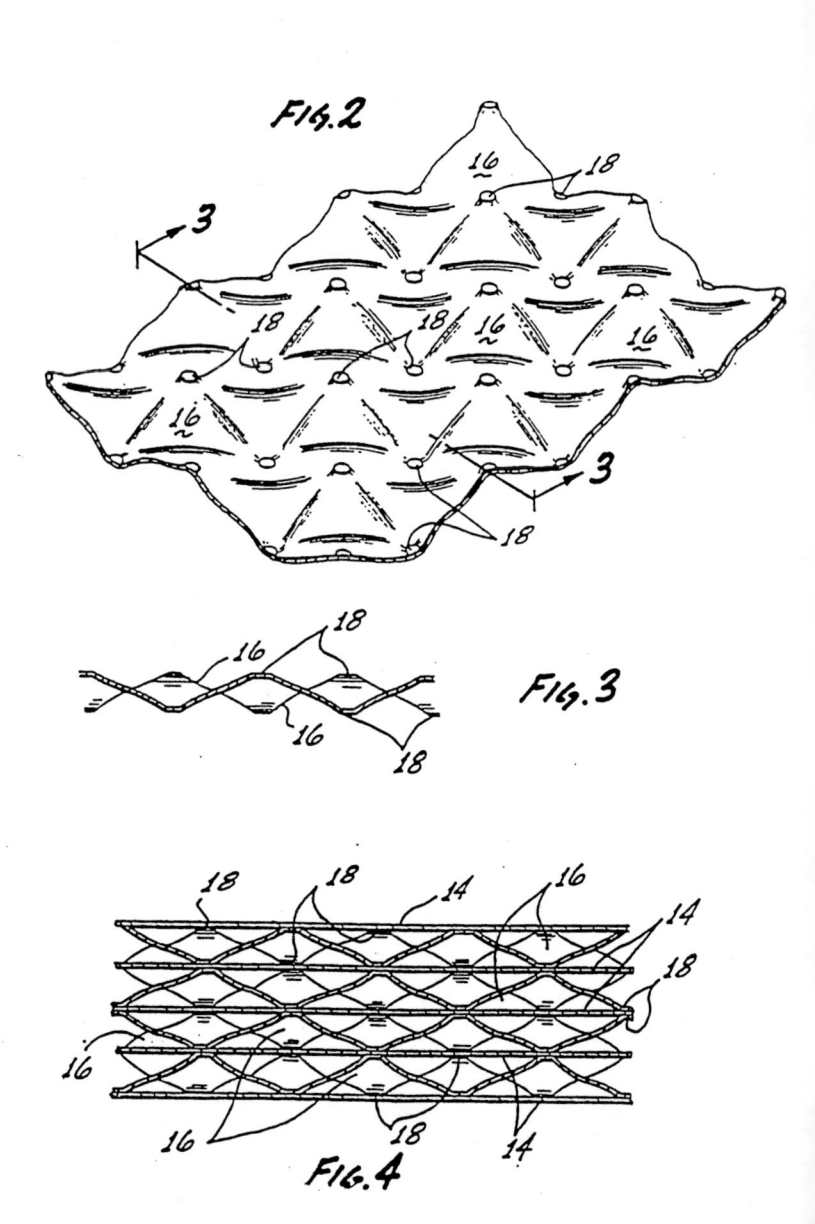

Fig. 3

Fig. 4

Process and Methods Patent for a mechanical, thermal barrier/heat transfer material for shield use.

approximately 3/8 of an inch being suitable for this purpose. Accordingly, Sibley et al disclose a device which reflects heat back toward its source rather than directing the heat from one portion of the heat insulating panel to another portion thereof
5   to thereby dissipate the heat.

U.S. Patent No. 1,934,174 ("Dyckerhoff") discloses a heat insulating body which includes a plurality of metal foil sheets which have been stamped, bent or crumpled to form projections which maintain the sheets in point contact when assembled in a
10 stack. Dyckerhoff discloses that the foil can be crumpled or distorted by hand or machine and applied to the surface of the member to be insulated, it being unnecessary to lock these sheets to each other to maintain the irregular shape necessary to provide thick air spaces. Dyckerhoff discloses that the average
15 spacing of the sheets can be about 1 cm but ordinarily will be between .5-2 cm, the sheets having a thickness which may be less than 0.2 mm and even as thin as 0.005 or thinner.

Dyckerhoff discloses that a protective casing can be provided to protect the insulation from outside pressures but
20 when the insulation is used for filling air spaces created by the usual structural members, such as walls or ceilings, no special casing is necessary whereas in the case of making pipe coatings, an outside shell which may be made of metal heavier than the foil is advisable. Dyckerhoff discloses that it is not necessary for
25 all of the sheets to be crumpled and the heat insulating body can include an intermediate sheet which remains flat. Dyckerhoff does not disclose any means for directing heat from one part of the insulating body to another part thereof.

U.S. Patent No. 2,926,761 ("Herbert, Jr."), U.S. Patent No.
30 4,343,866 ("Oser et al") and U.S. Patent No. 4,386,128

ABSTRACT

A pad including thermal insulation and heat sink areas. The pad includes a plurality of layers of metal foil forming a stack with the layers arranged one above the other, the stack including at least one heat sink area and at least one insulating area adjacent to the heat sink area, the layers providing better heat conduction in the vertical direction at the heat sink area than at the insulating area. At least one of the layers includes a plurality of embossments therein separating the one layer from an adjacent one of the layers in the insulating area. The pad can include a single insulating area surrounded by a heat sink area and a black coating can be provided on selected portions of the layers to improve heat radiating characteristics of the pad. For instance, the heat sink area can be coated with the black coating to radiate heat away from the pad at a desired location. The pad is particularly useful in shielding a heat sensitive component on one side of the pad from a heat source on the other side of the pad.

Process and Methods Patent for a mechanical, thermal barrier/heat transfer material f shield use.

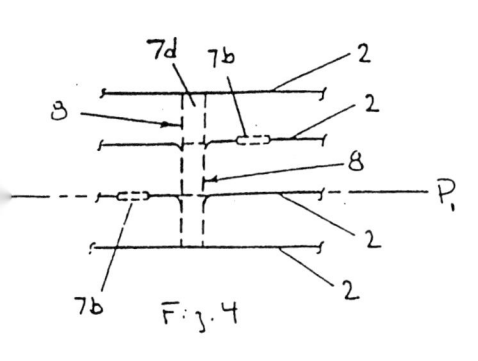

Fig. 4

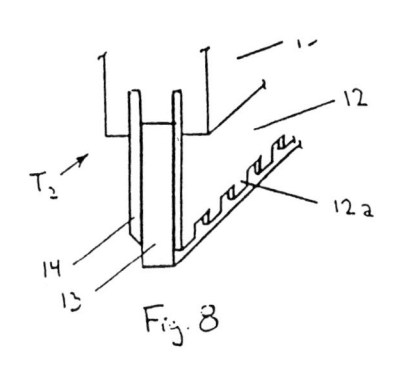

Fig. 8

Fig. 5

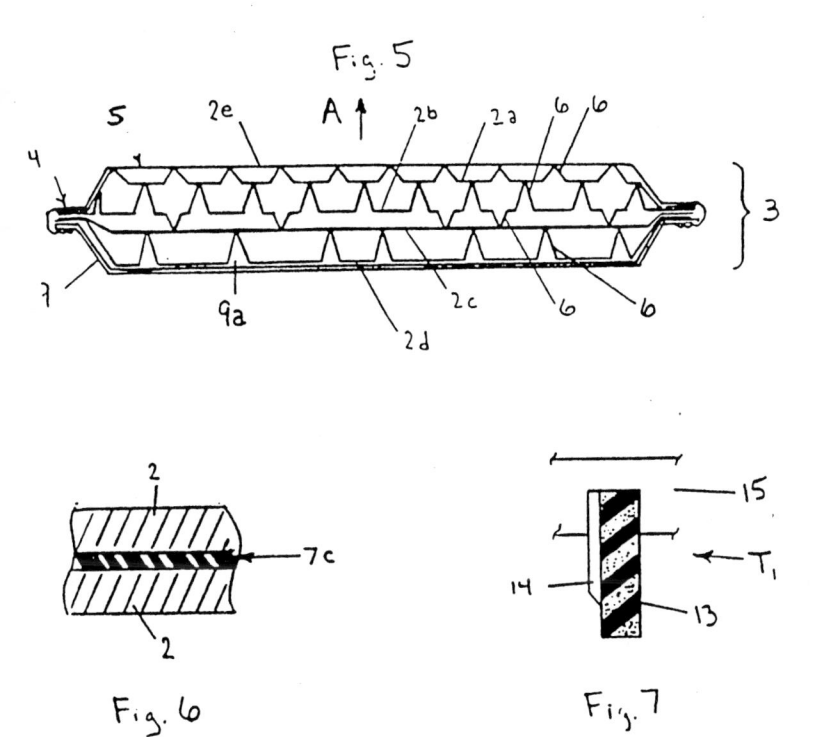

Fig. 6

Fig. 7

Process and Methods Patent for a mechanical, thermal barrier/heat transfer material for heat shield use.

Fig. 1

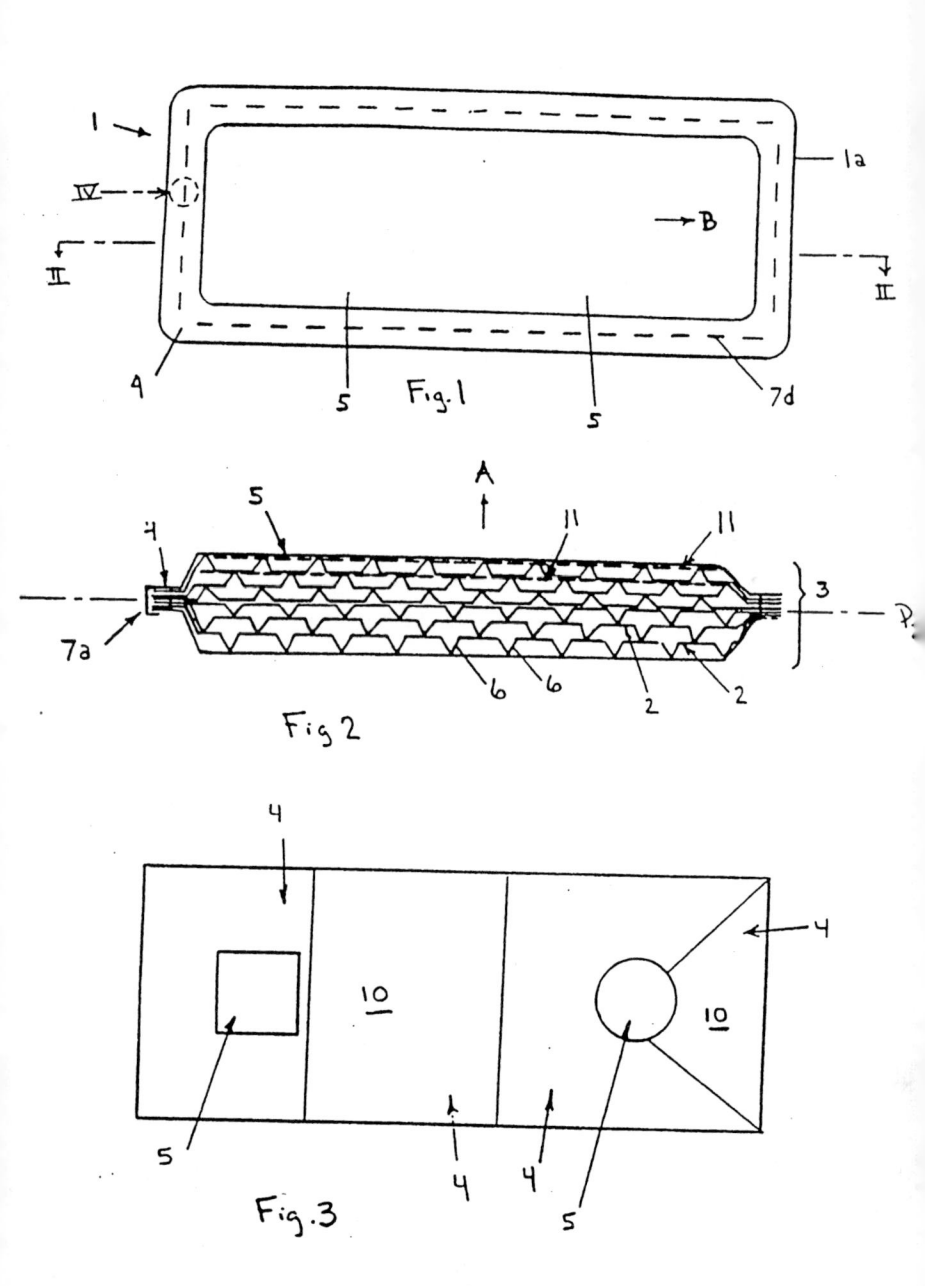

Fig. 2

Fig. 3

Process and Methods Patent for a mechanical, thermal barrier/heat transfer material for shield use.

United States Patent [19]

Daniels et al.

[11] Patent Number: 5,108,755
[45] Date of Patent: Apr. 28, 1992

[54] **BIODEGRADABLE COMPOSITES FOR INTERNAL MEDICAL USE**

[75] Inventors: Alma U. Daniels, Salt Lake City, Utah; Jorge Heller, Woodside, Calif.

[73] Assignees: SRI International, Menlo Park, Calif.; University of Utah, Salt Lake City, Utah

[21] Appl. No.: 345,034

[22] Filed: Apr. 27, 1989

[51] Int. Cl.⁵ A61F 2/00
[52] U.S. Cl. 424/426; 524/417; 424/78.37
[58] Field of Search 424/426, 78; 524/417

[56] **References Cited**

U.S. PATENT DOCUMENTS

3,640,741	2/1972	Etes	424/426 X
3,739,773	6/1973	Schmitt	424/426
4,093,709	6/1978	Choi et al.	424/426 X
4,096,239	6/1978	Katz et al.	424/426
4,304,767	12/1981	Heller et al.	424/78
4,346,028	8/1982	Griffith	524/417
4,513,143	4/1985	Ng et al.	549/335
4,532,335	7/1985	Helwing	549/335
4,639,366	1/1987	Heller	424/484
4,717,487	1/1988	Griffith et al.	252/1
4,764,364	8/1988	Heller et al.	424/78
4,786,664	11/1988	Yates	524/417

FOREIGN PATENT DOCUMENTS

0031223	7/1981	European Pat. Off.
0146398	6/1985	European Pat. Off
2169914	7/1986	United Kingdom

Primary Examiner—Thurman K. Page
Assistant Examiner—William E. Benston
Attorney, Agent, or Firm—Morrison & Foerster

[57] **ABSTRACT**

A family of composites suitable for use as materials of construction for implantable medical devices is disclosed. In the most preferred embodiment, the substrate polymer is an ortho ester polymer formed by the reaction of a ketene acetal having a functionality of two or more with a polyol. Also in the most preferred embodiment, the reinforcement material in the composites is calcium-sodium metaphosphate ("CSM") fibers. In other embodiments, the composites may replace either (but not both) of the substrate or the reinforcement with materials of the art.

10 Claims, 5 Drawing Sheets

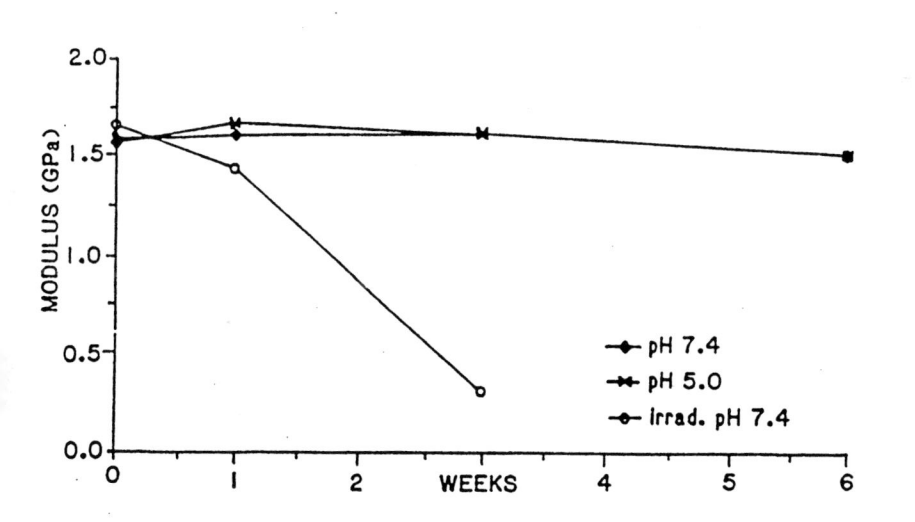

---

anical and Material Patent for a biomedical material invention wherein drawings
rate statistical information regarding performance of invention.   E-1

U.S. Patent   Apr. 28, 1992   Sheet 1 of 5   **5,108,75**

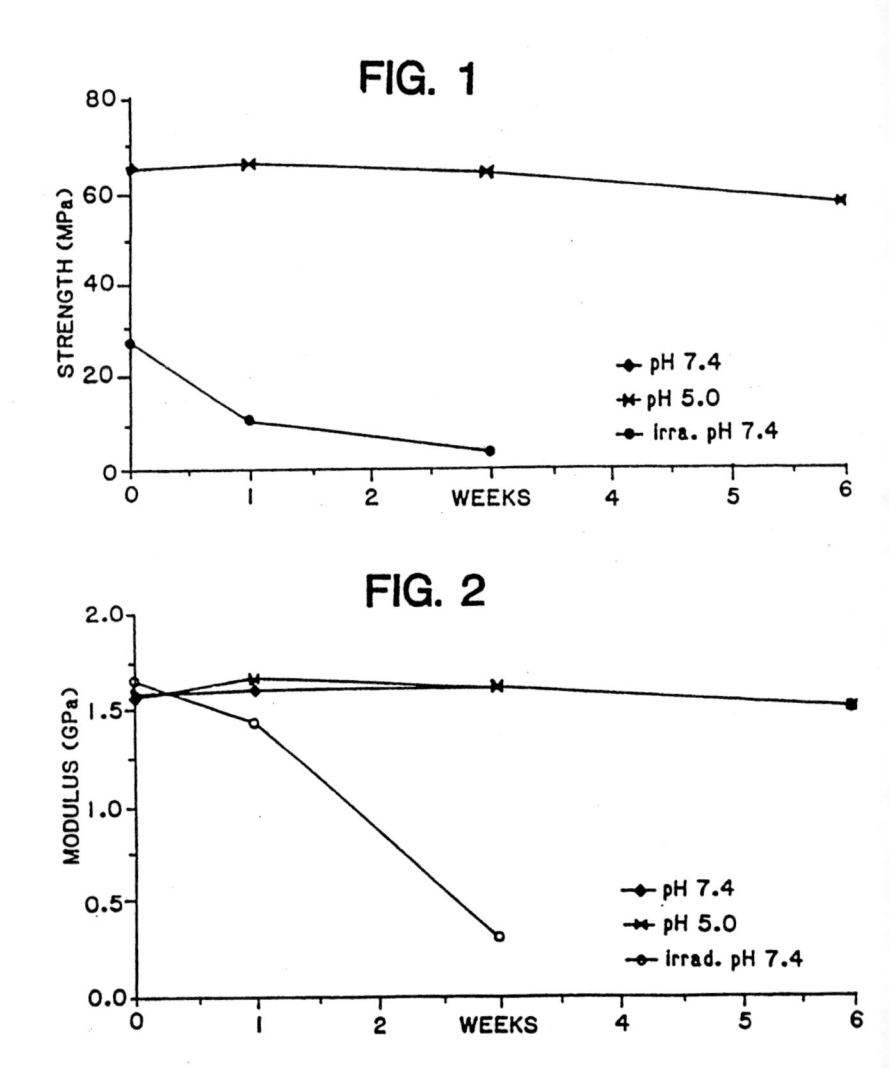

FIG. 1

FIG. 2

Mechanical and Material Patent for a biomedical material invention wherein dra illustrate statistical information regarding performance of invention.

FIG. 3a

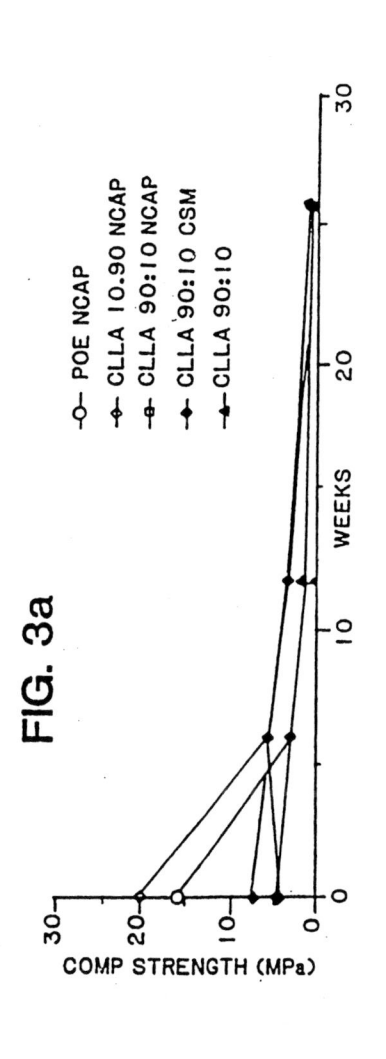

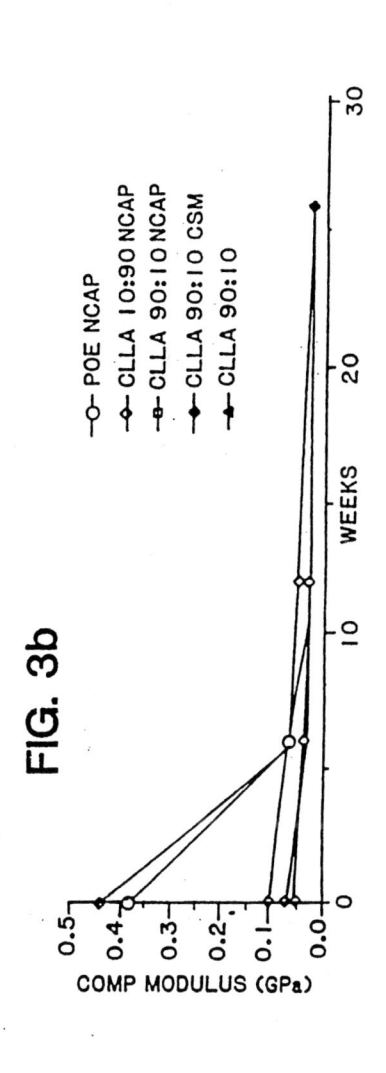

FIG. 3b

FIG. 4a

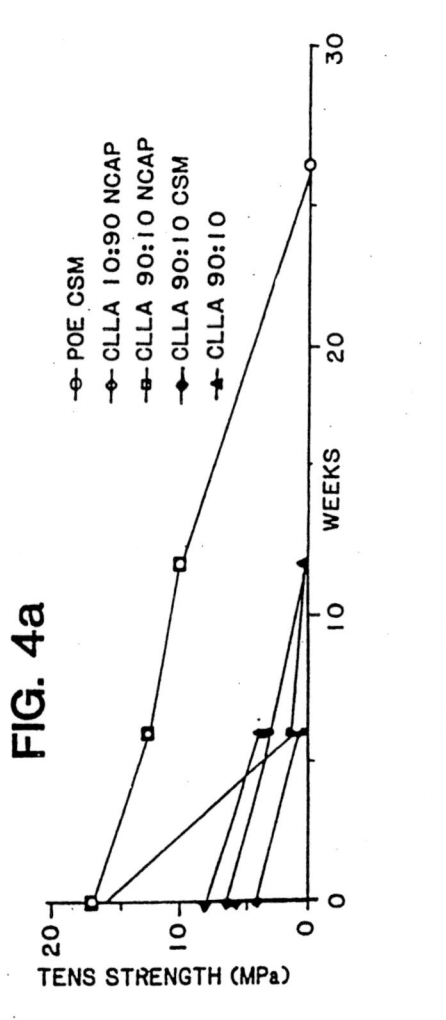

FIG. 4b

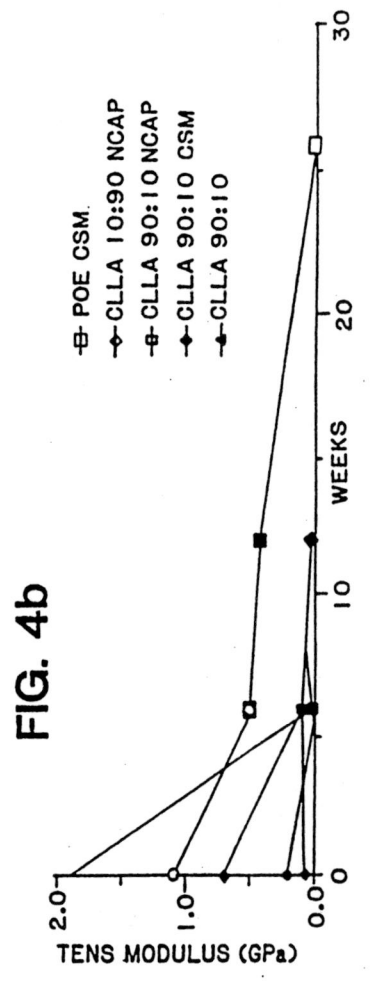

Mechanical and Material Patent for a biomedical material invention wherein drawings illustrate statistical information regarding performance of invention.

FIG. 5a

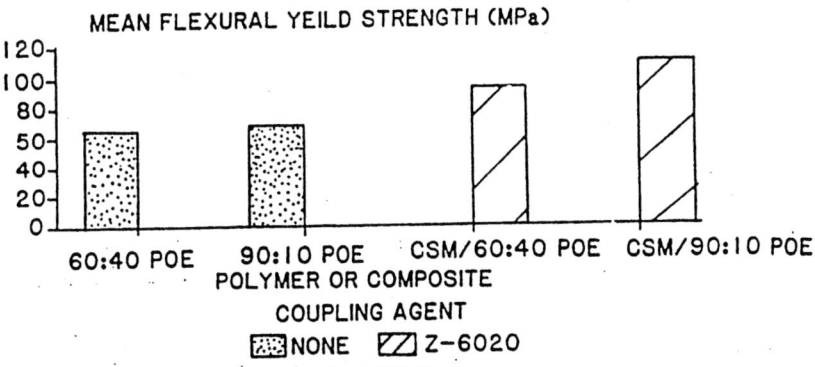

MEAN FLEXURAL YEILD STRENGTH (MPa)

[Bar chart showing values for 60:40 POE, 90:10 POE, CSM/60:40 POE, CSM/90:10 POE along POLYMER OR COMPOSITE axis]

COUPLING AGENT
NONE   Z-6020

60:40 POE AN COMPOSITE, T=130 C
90:10 POE AN COMPOSITE, T=180 C
Vf-30%, 0.3% COUPLING AGENT IN METHANOL

FIG. 5b

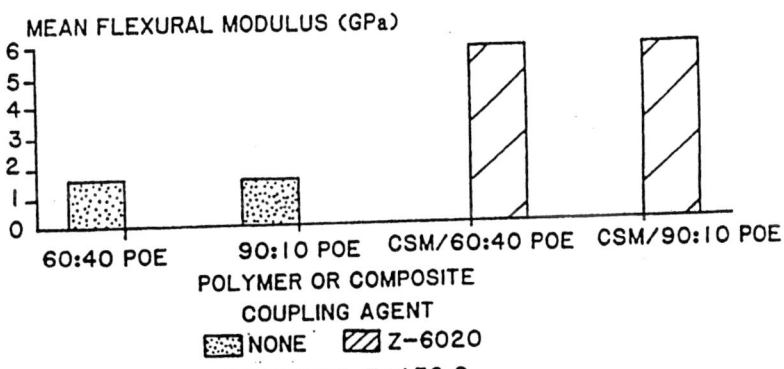

MEAN FLEXURAL MODULUS (GPa)

[Bar chart showing values for 60:40 POE, 90:10 POE, CSM/60:40 POE, CSM/90:10 POE along POLYMER OR COMPOSITE axis]

COUPLING AGENT
NONE   Z-6020

60:40 POE AND COMPOSITES, T=130 C
90:10 POE AND COMPOSITES, T=180 C
Vf-30%, 0.3% COUPLING AGENT IN METHANOL

FIG. 6a

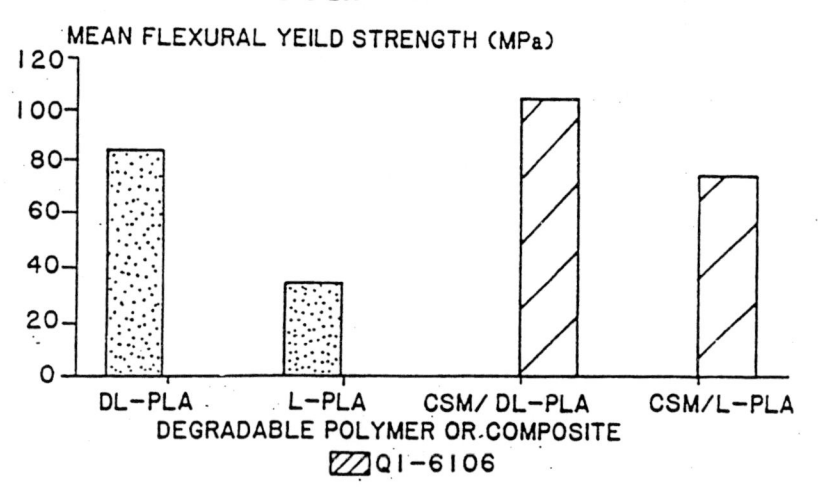

MEAN FLEXURAL YEILD STRENGTH (MPa)

DEGRADABLE POLYMER OR COMPOSITE

QI-6106

Vf-30%, 0.3% COUPLING AGENT IN METHANOL

FIG. 6b

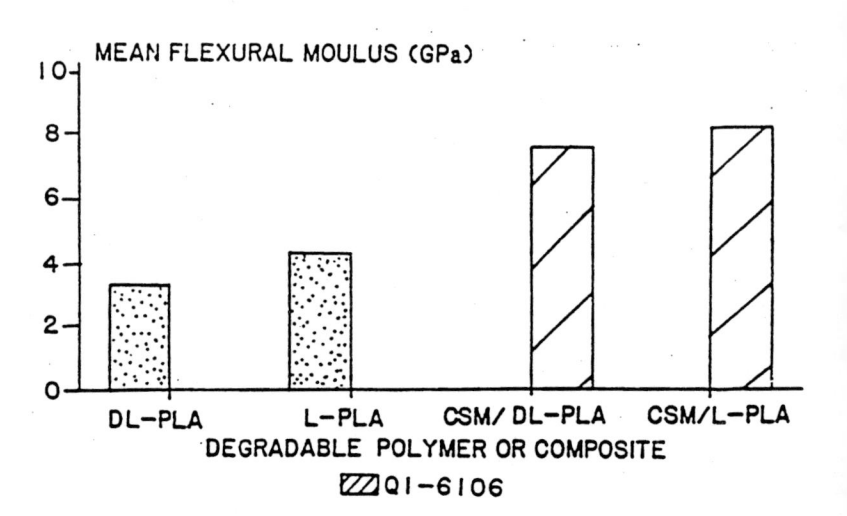

MEAN FLEXURAL MOULUS (GPa)

DEGRADABLE POLYMER OR COMPOSITE

QI-6106

Vf-30%, 0.3% COUPLING AGENT IN METHANOL

Mechanical and Material Patent for a biomedical material invention wherein draw illustrate statistical information regarding performance of invention.

United States Patent [19]
Tabor et al.

[11] Patent Number: 4,795,699
[45] Date of Patent: Jan. 3, 1989

[54] T7 DNA POLYMERASE

[75] Inventors: Stanley Tabor, Cambridge; Charles C. Richardson, Chestnut Hill, both of Mass.

[73] Assignee: President and Fellows of Harvard College, Cambridge, Mass.

[21] Appl. No.: 3,227

[22] Filed: Jan. 14, 1987

[51] Int. Cl.[4] C12Q 1/70; C12Q 1/68; C12N 15/00; C12P 19/34

[52] U.S. Cl. 435/5; 435/6; 435/91; 435/172.3; 435/803; 435/810; 935/77; 935/78

[58] Field of Search 435/5, 6, 91, 803, 172.3, 435/810; 436/501, 808; 935/78, 77

[56] References Cited

U.S. PATENT DOCUMENTS

3,444,041	5/1969	Spiegelman et al.	195/28
3,444,042	5/1969	Spiegelman et al.	195/28
3,661,893	5/1972	Spiegelman et al.	260/211.5
4,363,877	12/1982	Goodman et al.	435/317
4,483,920	11/1984	Gillespie et al.	
4,483,922	11/1984	Carpenter	
4,486,539	12/1984	Ranki et al.	
4,521,509	6/1985	Benkovic et al.	435/6
4,556,643	12/1985	Paau et al.	
4,563,419	1/1986	Ranki et al.	
4,591,565	5/1986	Brænner-Jorgensen	
4,656,127	4/1987	Mundy	435/6
4,663,283	5/1987	Kleid et al.	435/91
4,663,290	5/1987	Weis et al.	435/253
4,670,379	6/1987	Miller	435/6

OTHER PUBLICATIONS

nger, F. et al. *Proc. Natl. Acad. Sci. USA*, vol. 74, 1977 5463-5467.
at, J. et al. *Nucleic Acids Research*, vol. 5, 1978 pp. 37-4545.
Mills, D. R. et al., *Proc. Natl. Acad. Sci. USA*, vol. 76, 1979, pp. 2232-2235.
Studier, F. W. *Virology*, vol. 95, 1979, pp. 70-84.
Henning Jacobsen et al., "The N-Terminal Amino-Acid Sequences of DNA Polymerase I from *Escherichia coli* and of the Large and the Small Fragments Obtained by a Limited Proteolysis", *European Journal of Biochemistry*, vol. 45: 623, 1974.
Das, S. K. et al., *J. Biol. Chem.*, vol. 254, p. 1227, 1979.
McClure, W. R. et al., *J. Biol. Chem.*, vol. 250, p. 4073, 1975.
Bambara, R. A. et al., *J. Biol. Chem.*, vol. 253, p. 413, 1978.
Saiki, R. K. et al., *Science*, vol. 230, p. 1350, 1985.
Scharf et al., 23 *Science* 1076 (1986).
Tabor et al., In Thioredoxin and Glutaredoxin Systems: Structure and Function (Holmgren et al., ed) Raven Press, NY 285 (1986).
Barr et al., 4 *BioTechniques* 428 (1986).
Tabor et al., 82 *Proc. Natl. Acad. Sci.* 1074 (1985).
Russel et al., 82 *Proc. Natl. Acad. Sci.* 29 (1985).
Lim et al., 163 *J. Bacteriol.* 311 (1985).
Russel et al., 157 *J. of Bacteriol.* 526 (1984).
Lechner, R. L. et al., 258 *J. Biol. Chem.* 11174 (1983).
Lechner et al., 258 *J. Biol. Chem.* 11185 (1983).
Engler et al., 258 *J. Biol. Chem.* 11165 (1983).
DeBoer, 80 *Proc. Natl. Acad. Sci.* 21 (1983).
Fischer et al., 255 *J. Biol. Che.* 7956 (1980).
Adler et al., 254 *J. Biol. Chem.* 11605 (1979).
Hori et al., 254 *J. Biol. Chem.* 11598 (1979).
Mark et al., 73 *Proc. Natl. Acad. Sci.* 780 (1976).
Modrich et al., 250 *J. Biol. Chem.* 5515 (1975).
Lunn et al., 259 *J. Biol. Chem.* 10469 (1984).
Reutimann et al., 82 *Proc. Natl. Acad. Sci.* 6783 (1985).

Primary Examiner—Charles F. Warren
Assistant Examiner—Jeremy M. Jay

[57] ### ABSTRACT

This invention relates to T7-type DNA polymerases and method for using them.

32 Claims, 18 Drawing Sheets

U.S. Patent   Jan. 3, 1989   Sheet 1 of 18   4,795,6

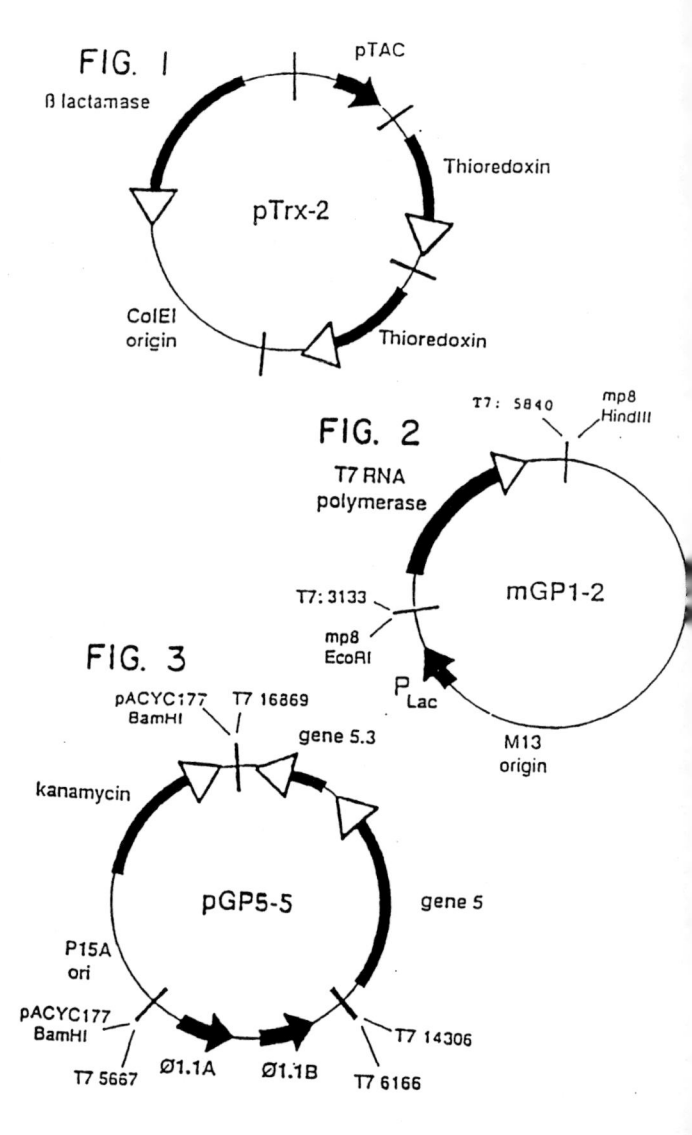

FIG. 1

pTrx-2: β lactamase, pTAC, Thioredoxin, Thioredoxin, ColEI origin

FIG. 2

mGP1-2: T7 RNA polymerase, T7: 5840, mp8 HindIII, T7: 3133, mp8 EcoRI, P Lac, M13 origin

FIG. 3

pGP5-5: pACYC177 BamHI, T7 16869, gene 5.3, kanamycin, gene 5, P15A ori, pACYC177 BamHI, T7 5667, Ø1.1A, Ø1.1B, T7 14306, T7 6166

Biotechnology and Methods Patent wherein the drawings show DNA Polymerase struct graphs and codes.

FIG. 4

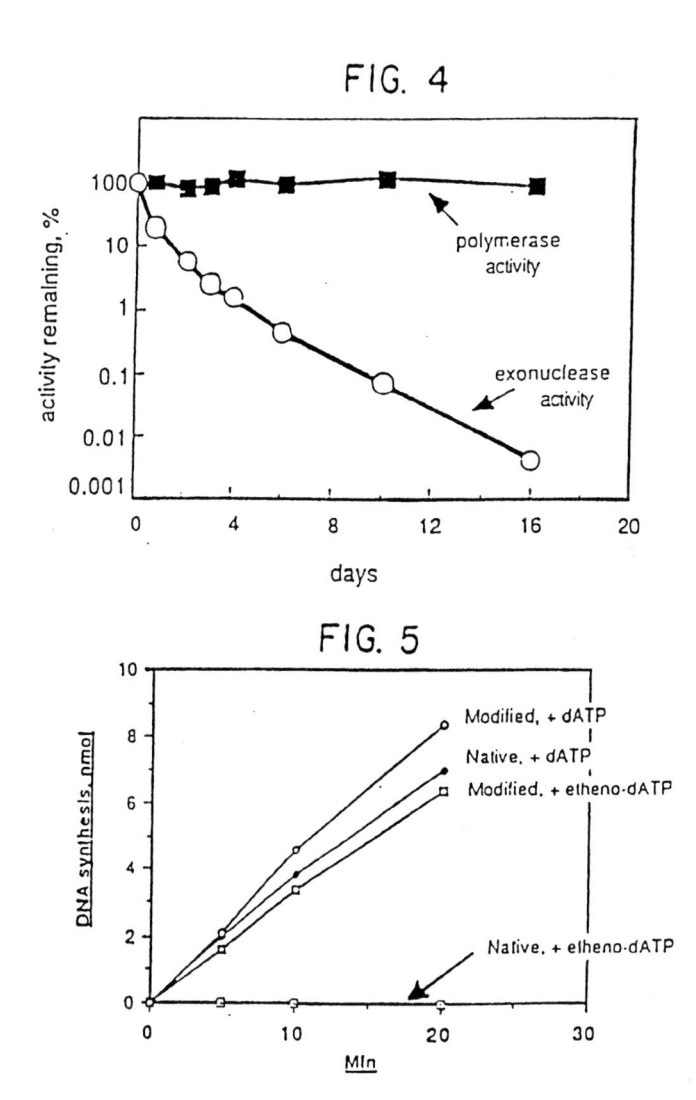

FIG. 5

FIG. 6

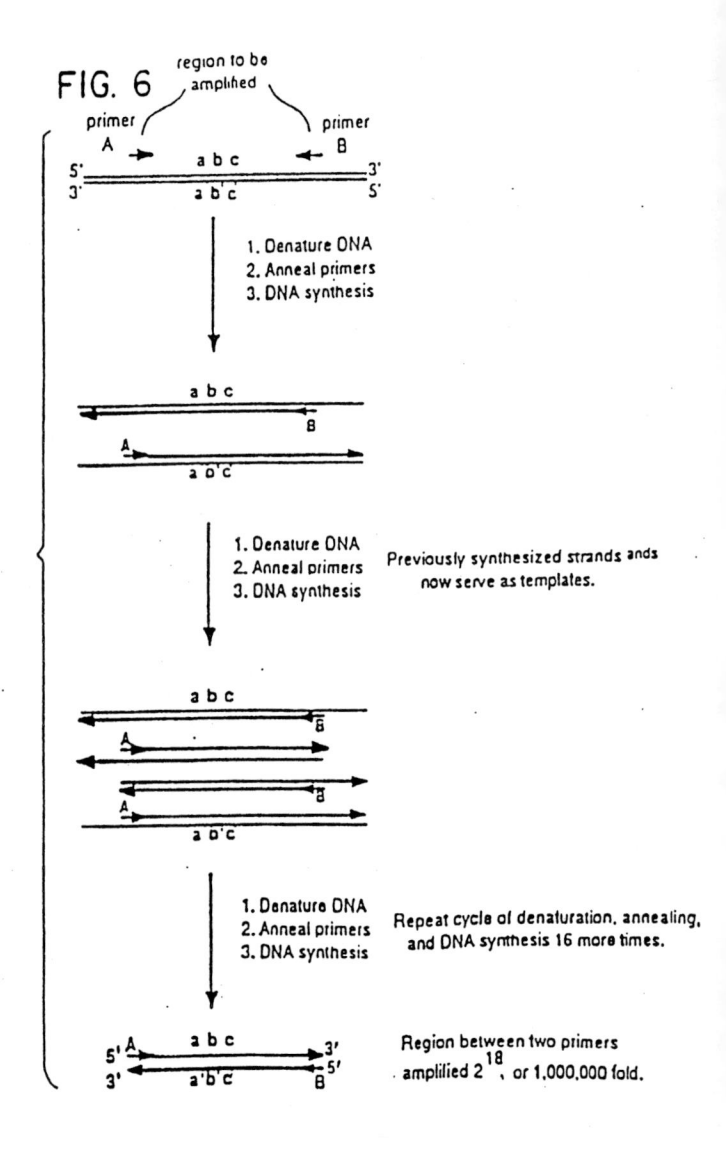

region to be amplified

primer A → a b c ← primer B
5'══════════════════════3'
3'══════a b'c══════════5'

↓ 1. Denature DNA
2. Anneal primers
3. DNA synthesis

a b c
←──────── B
A ────────→
a b'c

↓ 1. Denature DNA
2. Anneal primers
3. DNA synthesis

Previously synthesized strands and now serve as templates.

a b c
←──────── B
A ────────→
←──────── a
A ────────→
a b'c

↓ 1. Denature DNA
2. Anneal primers
3. DNA synthesis

Repeat cycle of denaturation, annealing, and DNA synthesis 16 more times.

5' A→   a b c   3'
3'   a'b'c   ←B 5'

Region between two primers amplified 2^{18}, or 1,000,000 fold.

Biotechnology and Methods Patent wherein the drawings show DNA Polymerase structure graphs and codes.

FIG. 7 -1

```
         10         20         30         40         50
    TTCTTCTCAT GTTTGACAGC TTATCATCGA CTGCACGGTG CACCAATGCT
         60         70         80         90        100
    TCTGGCGTCA GGCAGCCATC GGAAGCTGTG GTATGGCTGT GCAGGTCGTA
        110        120        130        140        150
    AATCACTGCA TAATTCGTGT CGCTCAAGGC GCACTCCCGT TCTGGATAAT
        160        170        180        190        200
    GTTTTTGCG CCGACATCAT AACGGTTCTG GCAAATATTC TGAAATGAGC
        210        220        230        240        250
    TGTTGACAAT TAATCATCGG CTCGTATAAT GTGTGGAATT GTGAGCGGAT
        260        270        280        290        300
    AACAATTTCA CACAGGAAAC AGGGGATCCG TCAACCTTTA GTTGGTTAAT
        310        320        330        340        350
    GTTACACCAA CAACGAAACC AACACGCCAG GCTTATTCCT GTGGAGTTAT
        360        370        380        390        400
    ATATGAGCGA TAAAATTATT CACCTGACTG ACGACAGTTT TGACACGGAT
        410        420        430        440        450
    GTACTCAAAG CGGACGGGGC GATCCTCGTC GATTTCTGGG CAGAGTGGTG
        460        470        480        490        500
    CGGTCCGTGC AAGATGATCG CCCCGATTCT GGATGAAATC GCTGACGAAT
```

FIG. 7-2

```
      510        520        530        540        550
ATCAGGGCAA ACTGACCGTT GCAAAACTGA ACATCGATCA AAACCCTGGT
      560        570        580        590        600
ACTGCGCCGA AATATGGCAT CCGTGGTATC CCGACTCTGC TGCTGTTCAA
      610        620        630        640        650
AAACGGTGAA GTGGCGGCAA CCAAAGTGGG TGCACTGTCT AAAGGTCAGT
      660        670        680        690        700
TGAAAGAGTT CCTCGACGCT AACCTGGCGT AAGGGAATTT CATGTTCGGG
      710        720        730        740        750
TGCCCCGTCG CTAAAACTG GACGCCCGGC GTGAGTCATG CTAACTTAGT
      760        770        780        790        800
GTTGACGGAT CCCCGGGAT CCGTCAACCT TTAGTTGGTT AATGTTACAC
      810        820        830        840        850
CAACAACGAA ACCAACACGC CAGGCTTATT CCTGTGGAGT TATATATGAG
      860        870        880        890        900
CGATAAAATT ATTCACCTGA CTGACGACAG TTTTGACACG GATGTACTCA
      910        920        930        940        950
AAGCGGACGG GGCGATCCTC GTCGATTTCT GGGCAGAGTG GTGCGGTCCG
      960        970        980        990       1000
TGCAAGATGA TCGCCCCGAT TCTGGATGAA ATCGCTGACG AATATCAGGG
     1010       1020       1030       1040       1050
CAAACTGACC GTTGCAAAAC TGAACATCGA TCAAAACCCT GGTACTGCGC
     1060       1070       1080       1090       1100
CGAAATATGG CATCCGTGGT ATCCCGACTC TGCTGCTGTT CAAAAACGGT
     1110       1120       1130       1140       1150
GAAGTGGCGG CAACCAAAGT GGGTGCACTG TCTAAAGGTC AGTTGAAAGA
     1160       1170       1180       1190       1200
GTTCCTCGAC GCTAACCTGG CGTAAGGGAA TTTCATGTTC GGGTGCCCCG
     1210       1220       1230       1240       1250
TCGCTAAAAA CTGGACGCCC GGCGTGAGTC ATGCTAACTT AGTGTTGACG
     1260       1270       1280       1290       1300
GATCCCCCTG CCTCGCGCGT TTCGGTGATG ACGGTGAAAA CCTCTGACAC
     1310       1320       1330       1340       1350
ATGCAGCTCC CGGAGACGGT CACAGCTTGT CTGTAAGCGG ATGCCGGGAG
     1360       1370       1380       1390       1400
CAGACAAGCC CGTCAGGGCG CGTCAGCGGG TGTTGGCGGG TGTCGGGGCG
     1410       1420       1430       1440       1450
CAGCCATGAC CCAGTCACGT AGCGATAGCG GAGTGTATAC TGGCTTAACT
     1460       1470       1480       1490       1500
ATGCGGCATC AGAGCAGATT GTACTGAGAG TGCACCATAT GCGGTGTGAA
     1510       1520       1530       1540       1550
ATACCGCACA GATGCGTAAG GAGAAAATAC CGCATCAGGC GCTCTTCCGC
     1560       1570       1580       1590       1600
TTCCTCGCTC ACTGACTCGC TGCGCTCGGT CGTTCGGCTG CGGCGAGCGG
     1610       1620       1630       1640       1650
TATCAGCTCA CTCAAAGGCG GTAATACGGT TATCCACAGA ATCAGGGGAT
     1660       1670       1680       1690       1700
AACGCAGGAA AGAACATGTG AGCAAAAGGC CAGCAAAAGG CCAGGAACCG
     1710       1720       1730       1740       1750
TAAAAAGGCC GCGTTGCTGG CGTTTTTCCA TAGGCTCCGC CCCCCTGACG
     1760       1770       1780       1790       1800
AGCATCACAA AAATCGACGC TCAAGTCAGA GGTGGCGAAA CCCGACAGGA
     1810       1820       1830       1840       1850
CTATAAAGAT ACCAGGCGTT TCCCCCTGGA AGCTCCCTCG TGCGCTCTCC
```

304,407
BEVERAGE DISPENSER
Gregory Fossella, Boston, Mass., assignor to Jet Spray Corp., Norwood, Mass.
Filed Jun. 12, 1986, Ser. No. 873,338
Term of patent 14 years
U.S. Cl. D7—308

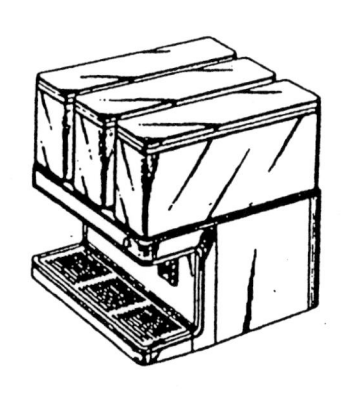

304,266
SOFA
Richard Frinier, Long Beach, Calif., assignor to Brown Jordan Company, El Monte, Calif.
Filed Jul. 3, 1985, Ser. No. 752,240
The portion of the term of this patent subsequent to Jul. 5, 2002, has been disclaimed.
Term of patent 14 years
U.S. Cl. D6—381

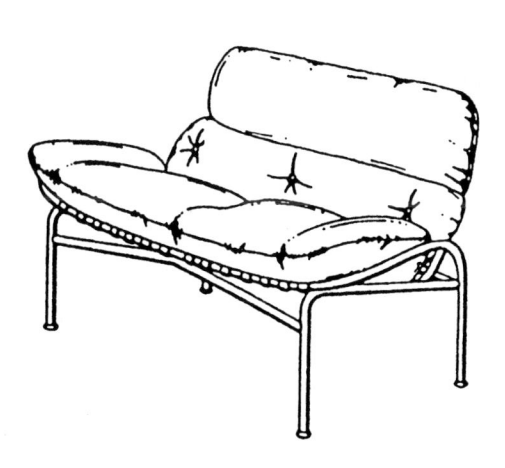

---

sign Patents. Although these inventions may have utility, their functions are separate
n their design. A claim in a design patent application for utility or functionality will
clude acceptance of a design patent application.

License or Sale Checklist
Am I Ready to Sell or License?

The following items are intended only as general questions to help maximize the sale or licensing of intellectual property. Professional advice should be sought since one project may have needs which might differ from another project.

1. Have I had a contract attorney and/or an intellectual property attorney review the documents?
2. If time is of the essence, are dates and times listed in a clear and specific manner? Are there written projected time tables for the various stages?
3. Do I know the financial condition of the company? Have I had an accountant review the past two years of the licensing or purchasing company's financial statements and the financial terms of the agreement?
4. Does the licensing or purchasing company have any litigation pending which could jeopardize all resources earmarked for my project and delay the development of my project?
5. Are there clearly enumerated dollar amounts available to complete and bring the project to completion?
6. Are my royalties or sale proceeds based on "net" or "gross" sales? If on "net," are there caps on expenses or only specific costs included in calculating net sales?
7. Is there a possible conflict of interest in the primary business of the company which would delay getting my project to the marketplace?

8. Do I have a copy of the corporate resolution committing the company to purchase or license my project?
9. Do I have my documentation for the project complete and in order, to counter any future contests of rights or ownership?
10. Have I considered liability questions and protected my interests, including a recovery of technoloy provision from the licensing company if the project is not successful?
11. Does the agreement contain a provision for dealing with infringers? Is there a "noncompete" clause?
12. Are all initial project funds deposited in an escrow account for efficient transition of funds before signing documents?
13. Have I considered confidentiality issues so that I protect my proprietary technology and trade secrets.
14. Do I have confidence that my advisors are "helping me," rather than "helping themselves" to my assets?
15. Am I mentally and emotionally prepared to complete the transactions?

"Move in Haste, Repent in Leisure!"

Invention Works
Develop, Protect And
Make Money On Your Invention

Richard Crangle

Richard Crangle is the founder and president of **Crantec Research**, a research and development company for innovative products. He is an adjunct professor at the University of Utah and Salt Lake Community College and has been a faculty member at Augustana College and Creighton University. He has also worked for several governmental agencies, private firms and large corporations.

Through Crantec Research, Richard has invented, researched and developed many proprietary technology devices. He has been a co-inventor for several innovative technologies and produced, marketed and distributed products over a 15-year period. In the area of technology innovation, he is a veteran and has experienced success and loss, both of which contribute to a balanced and measured treatment of the technology innovation business and the patent process.

In addition to technology consulting, Richard also conducts workshops for members of universities, associations, and business development groups who wish to obtain a better understanding of the many facets of technology development.

> The author expresses appreciation to Beverly Crangle and admiration for her considerable editorial skills and talents which brought this work to a much higher level than could have been achieved without her assistance.

Your Comments and Suggestions Are Welcomed!

In order to make *Invention Works* the best tool for you and others, your assistance is needed in telling us what has been the most beneficial or least beneficial about this book for you.

What information would you like to see included?

_____

_____

Is there anything you feel should have been excluded?

_____

_____

Would you recommend this book to others?
☐ Yes   ☐ No
If so, to whom:

_____

Please write down your comments and suggestions and mail to:

Crantec Research
300 Sports Mall Plaza I
5505 So. 900 E.
Salt Lake City, UT 84117

Thank you for taking the time to complete and mail this to us!